WRITE WAYS
MODELLING WRITING FORMS

Lesley Wing Jan

bourne

OXFORD UNIVERSITY PRESS

OXFORD UNIVERSITY PRESS AUSTRALIA

Oxford New York
Athens Auckland Bangkok Bombay
Calcutta Cape Town Dar es Salaam Delhi
Florence Hong Kong Istanbul Karachi
Kuala Lumpur Madras Madrid Melbourne
Mexico City Nairobi Paris Port Moresby
Singapore Taipei Tokyo Toronto

and associated companies in
Berlin Ibadan

OXFORD is a trade mark of Oxford University Press

National Library of Australia
Cataloguing-in-Publication data:

Wing Jan, Leslie
   Write ways: modelling writing forms.

   ISBN 0 19 553202 3.

   1. English language — Composition and
   excercises — Study and teaching (Primary).
   2. Language arts (Primary). I. Title

372.6044

Typeset by Solo Typesetting, South Australia
Printed through Bookpac Production Services, Singapore
Published by Oxford University Press,
253 Normanby Road, South Melbourne, Australia

CONTENTS

INTRODUCTION

▼

This book has been written with the intention of providing teachers with an easy-to-read resource for some of the many forms of writing we use to meet our needs. It provides suggestions for activities to help children develop an understanding of the writing process and of the purposes and structures of the many writing forms. There are ideas for programme planning as well as assessment and evaluation strategies.

Each section includes a description of a particular writing form so that the teacher is clear about its characteristics. Following the description there are suggested learning experiences that can be planned to help the children understand the structure and function of the writing form being modelled. Oral, written and reading activities are included for each writing form. A check-list for each writing form is also included and these can be used to help teachers formulate their programme objectives as well as for the assessment of the children.

At the end of each section a sample Unit of Work based on a single book or several books has been included to provide a practical framework for teachers attempting to emphasise the links between reading and writing. The Units of Work are planned to focus on the function and structure of texts so the many other potentials of these books are not included.

The information in this book has not been arranged in the order needed to be taught; rather, it is hoped that teachers will select relevant sections appropriate to their children's writing needs or to the content area of their classroom programmes.

1

LEARNING ABOUT LANGUAGE

Purposes of language

The focus of language teaching should be to provide children with authentic and relevant purposes for using language. Through these meaningful interactions the children will develop a control of language that is functional and purposeful in meeting their immediate and future needs.

Teachers need to know the many purposes of language, and the appropriate writing form to meet each purpose, so that they can provide the children with suitable models of written language. Teachers also need to know the structure and features of each writing form so that they can intervene in the children's learning cycle as the need arises.

Table 1.1 provides a framework for a range of purposes to write listed with the relevant forms of writing. Table 1.2 contains the main demonstration books used in this book and illustrates how these can be used to model the purposes of language and some of the writing forms outlined in the previous table.

Conditions for literacy learning

Although there are many different ways that children learn language it has been suggested that certain conditions are essential for literacy learning. These are set out on pages 4 and 5.

Table 1.1: Purposes to write and the relevant forms

Purpose	Writing Form
To record feelings, observations, etc.	Personal letters Science reports Poems Jottings of sensory impressions from observations, stories, drama, music, art Diaries Journals
To describe	Character portraits Reports of a sequence of events Labels and captions Advertisements, e.g. Wanted to Buy or Sell, Lost and Found
To inform or advise	Posters advertising coming events Scripts for news broadcasts Minutes of meetings Invitations Programs
To persuade	Advertisements and commercials Letters to the editor Notes for a debate Cartoons
To clarify thinking	Note-taking for research topics Explanations of graphs, science diagrams, etc. Jottings
To explore and maintain relationships with others	Letters Making requests Greeting cards Questionnaires
To predict or hypothesise	Speculations about probable outcomes in health, science, social studies topics Endings for stories Questions for research or interviews
To make comparisons	Charts Note-making Diagrams, graphs Descriptions
To command or direct	Recipes Instructions. How to make a . . . Stage directions Rules for games, safety, health, etc.
To amuse or entertain	Jokes, riddles, puzzles Scripts for drama, puppet plays Stories and poems Personal anecdotes

Source: *Writing: R–7 Lanaguage Arts* pp. 17–18.

Table 1.2: Demonstration books used in this book

Text Types	Purposes of language demonstrated	Writing forms which could be demonstrated
Reports: *Five Trees*	inform clarify thinking describe make comparisons record observations	science reports note-taking descriptions labels & captions charts diagrams
Procedural texts: *Kids in the Kitchen*	command or direct describe	rules instructions recipes diagrams explanations speculation
Explanations: *Down Roundabout and Up Again*	describe inform clarify thinking make comparisons record observations	note-taking diagrams descriptions labels explanations speculation
Persuasive writing: *A Pet for Mrs Arbuckle*	amuse & entertain persuade describe	story ending for story descriptions speculation about outcomes outcomes character portraits advertisements
The Animal Question	inform persuade clarify thinking compare hypothesise	note-taking for research topics letters speculation descriptions
Recounts: *Coming Home A Dog's True Story*	inform & describe amuse & entertain record feelings & observations	science reports diaries journals sequence of events stories
Narrative information: *Longneck's Billabong*	amuse & entertain clarify thinking compare inform	story sequence of events descriptions questions for research note-taking
Modern fiction: *Wilfrid Gordon McDonald Partridge* *Felix and Alexander*	describe amuse & entertain explore and maintain relationships make comparisons predict	story ending for story prediction speculation about outcomes

continued over page

Table 1.2: *Continued*

Text Types	Purposes of language demonstrated	Writing forms which could be demonstrated
Traditional fiction: folk-tales: *Red Riding Hood* *Little Red Riding Hood* myths & legends: *Pheasant and Kingfisher* *The Girl Who Loved Horses* fables: *The Lion and the Rat* *The Hare and the Tortoise* *The Rich Man and the Shoemaker* *The Miller, the Boy and the Donkey* *Fables*	amuse entertain inform describe make comparisons predict	stories parodies endings for stories descriptions comparisons scripts for drama character portraits

Immersion

The selection, display and reading to and by the children of good quality writing forms.

Demonstration

The implicit and explicit modelling of writing forms enables the children to understand the purpose and structure of texts.

Expectation

The teacher, through implicit and explicit modelling, expects the children to gain understanding from the experiences. The children, through the supportive climate in the classroom, expect to use the knowledge they've gained about writing forms.

Responsibility

The nature of the programme allows the children to take from the modelling sessions what is appropriate to their language development and needs at the time. The children, through greater knowledge of writing forms, are empowered to make more informed choices when they are writing.

Use

The writing forms are introduced in meaningful contexts which enable the children to practise and develop their skills in authentic situations.

Approximation

The children are encouraged in their attempts at writing in a selected form. Even though the children's first efforts may only include rudiments of the actual writing form, it is recognised that they are developing as competent writers.

Response

The share times at the conclusion of activity periods, conference times and group discussions provide opportunities for the children to try out their ideas and knowledge on an audience consisting of peers and an informed adult. The teacher is able to provide feedback in a supportive classroom climate.

Engagement

Once the learners have made the connections between the modelled texts and the desirability to use this writing form themselves they are actively involved in the learning process. They interact with the teacher and peers to explore their further learning possibilities within a supportive classroom environment.

What is modelling?

In this book the term 'modelling' is used to mean the planned and incidental exploitation of opportunities to introduce children to the purposes, structure and function of various writing forms. It also incorporates an adaptation of the approach to teaching writing in which the term 'modelling' means the development of children's knowledge of written language through both the implicit approach of reading to, with and by children of various writing forms and the explicit approach of composing a writing form for, with or by the children to show them how it is constructed.

Texts can be constructed in front of the children using:
- the overhead projector so that the text is clearly visible to the class as it is being written
- the chalkboard
- large sheets of paper which can be hung on the wall in view of the children and the texts can be written on these.

Both planned and incidental modelling opportunities can include implicit and explicit modelling.

Planned modelling opportunities

Planned modelling opportunities may include:

- The teacher's selection of a particular text based on the teaching focus she wishes to develop and the planned reading and analysis of the text with the children. This provides an implicit model of the writing form. For example: the teacher may select and read to the children a range of reports to introduce them to the structure and uses of language within these. The reports are read to the children as a planned activity in which the children are able to hear the patterns of language in reports.
- The teacher's planned demonstration of how to write a particular writing form through the construction, in front of the children, of a desired writing form. This provides explicit modelling of the writing form. For example: the teacher may wish to explain the features of report writing by actually constructing this form in front of the children and discussing the structure and process as the report is written.

Implicit and explicit modelling + constructing a text or front of/with children

Incidental modelling opportunities

Incidental modelling opportunities may include:

- The casual selection of and reading to the children of any text. This provides implicit modelling of written language. For example: the teacher may read books brought to school by the students. The reading of these presents the children with patterns of language.
- The construction of texts which arise incidentally out of classroom activities provide explicit modelling of the writing form if the teacher discusses the structure as it is written. For example: a notice about a class activity may need to be sent home to the parents. The teacher writes the notice in front of the children and discusses its construction as it is written. This is not a planned modelling session but arises incidentally out of the day's activities.

    Modelling is a powerful way of demonstrating: → *Why model?*
- how authors go about writing
- how they plan for their writing
- how they work and rework their writing
- how they go about solving spelling, punctuation and grammatical problems
- how different writing forms are used for different purposes and audiences.

    Modelling enables the teacher to focus the children's attention on different writing forms and to develop a shared language to use when they are interacting with these texts.

what modelling develops.

Modelling helps children recognise and identify features of texts which indicate their purpose.

Observing & classifying

↓

helps them become independent learners/writers!

The implicit and explicit modelling of both factual and narrative texts enables the children to learn how our language is structured for different purposes. Through modelling, children can be encouraged to consider the following:

◆ What was the author's intent in writing the text?
◆ What would the author need to know before writing the text?
◆ How was the information organised?
◆ How did the author write the text?
◆ How was the content arranged?
◆ Who was the target audience for the writing?
◆ What publishing conventions and formats have been used in the book?

Modelling empowers the children to observe, discover, classify and organise their knowledge about written language and then apply this knowledge to their own personal reading and writing, without the need for formal skills lessons or exercises that are isolated from the children's writing.

Once the children have become familiar with the structure of different forms of writing used for different purposes and audiences they can select the appropriate form for their writing needs.

As many of the writing forms are not a well developed part of the child's repertoire (for example persuasive writing) they need to be specifically demonstrated, through implicit and explicit modelling, so they are able to make informed choices on the form of language they wish to use to meet their particular writing needs.

The shared book experience

One way of modelling is to use shared book experiences. In this book the term 'shared book' refers to the shared reading, exploration, discussion and enjoyment of a book whose text is fully visible to both teacher and children. It may involve the use of a big book placed in view of all the participants or the use of multiple copies of a book, of which both the teacher and the children have a copy.

Shared book experiences provide the children with opportunities to explore various writing forms within a supportive climate; one in which all participants can help to add to the pool of knowledge about the text under the guidance of the teacher. These shared book experiences are invaluable in developing an understanding of the many different forms of writing used for different purposes and audiences and how these forms are structured. The children must be able to identify the purpose of and audience for their own writing so that they are able to write in the appropriate form.

2

ORGANISATION, PLANNING AND MANAGEMENT

▼

Role of the teacher

The teacher is the most important component in the success of the language programme regardless of the resources or commercial programmes available. The teacher must assume the role of facilitator or manager of the children's learning and be able to intervene in the learning process when 'teachable moments' occur. This is a very important responsibility in the teaching and learning of different writing forms; the teacher must plan and model appropriate writing forms in a meaningful context as the need arises within either the individual, group or class.

facilitator of learning

Plan and model } important

A successful language teacher must involve the children in authentic language activities, listen to them and respond according to their needs. The teacher must demonstrate how language is used and share the technical aspects of the writing process with the children. Above all, the teacher must assume responsibility for the planning of a well balanced language programme in which the children are active participants and are empowered with control over their own writing.

The following points may help define the responsibilities of the teacher in the context of teaching writing forms.

- Be familiar with the different purposes and forms of language.
- Model the many different forms of writing.
- Plan the language programme to include a variety of narrative and factual writing styles.
- Provide the best possible models of the different writing forms.
- Draw language activities from the content areas of the curriculum.

- Be aware of the unique uses of language within each subject area and model these.
- Understand the writing process and provide models of this to show how writers choose their topics, plan, research, write and rewrite, edit and publish their writing.
- Generate curiousity and interest in all forms of writing through planned and incidental activities and discussions that explore the structure of texts.
- Provide opportunities for the children to write every day. This may be in the form of diary writing, personal writing, jointly constructed writing or writing within the content area.
- Take every opportunity to link reading with writing. For example: when reading to the children use opportunities to discuss the texts as writers. When writing a text talk about it as readers.
- Formulate firm objectives for the writing programme. For example:
  ▷ The children will explore the structure and purpose of a variety of writing forms.
  ▷ The writing forms will be drawn from authentic sources, etc.
- Establish a classroom environment that encourages risk-taking and experimentation.
- Devise and use appropriate evaluation strategies for:
  ▷ the programme
  ▷ the children's progress
  ▷ your performance
  ▷ the resources used.

Set up displays of children's writing in its many stages.

- Keep cumulative, dated samples of the children's work and regular anecdotal records of conferences to help with pupil assessment.
- Provide the expectation that all children will become better writers.
- Establish a classroom environment that immerses the children in the many forms of writing. For example:
  ▷ Display books—both fiction and factual.
  ▷ Set up displays of children's writing in its many stages from draft form to published writing.
  ▷ Provide charts, signs and posters around the room. Provide reading and writing centres.
- Provide display areas for the children's writing as well as for published texts.
- Know when to intervene to develop an individual's, a group's or the class's writing knowledge.
- Understand that it takes time for the children to produce work of a high standard.
- Allow time for the children's personal reading and writing on topics of their own choice as well as their writing across the curriculum.

- Continue with professional reading and development to make sure you are aware of current educational research findings and their implications for teaching practice.

....

Classroom organisation

The children will be involved in a range of activities so it is important to arrange the room to provide space for individual, small group and whole class activities as well as to facilitate easy teacher and pupil movement around the room. Sufficient floor space or room needs to be made available to enable the whole class to be seated close together for modelling or focus sessions and share-time activities.

Ways to create a stimulating classroom environment

- Make sure the seating is arranged so that the children are able to work together easily.
- Store the children's writing and reading requirements within their reach.
- Set up a classroom library that includes a wide range of reading materials. Both commercially published and class constructed books can be included in the collection. It should include fiction and factual books that incorporate various writing forms.
- Allocate space for occasional displays of those books that include the writing form or the topic being explored at the time.
- Write signs to draw the children's attention to the various ways books are written. For example:
  ▷ What did the author need to know to write this book?
  ▷ How was the information arranged in this book?
  ▷ Why are these books similar/different?
- Try to display books so that the covers are face out to tempt the children to pick them up to read.
- Provide a range of resource and reference books. Have a selection of different dictionaries, thesauri, etc. easily accessible to the children.
- Set up a big-book stand or an art easel (to serve as a book stand) in the part of the room that is to be used for modelling or share time activities.
- Place the chalkboard, whiteboard or an art easel (with large sheets of paper attached) so that the whole class can see it during modelled writing activities.
- Create a print-enriched environment that will demonstrate the many ways we use written language. Use books, charts, labels,

Creating a print-enriched environment immerses the children in the many forms and purposes of written language.

signs, instructions, children's work, posters, schedules, time-tables, wallstories etc. to immerse the children in print.

- Start a class-book that will include information on the forms of writing as they are discovered by the children. It can include an explanation of the form plus examples from magazines, the children's writing and from the children's literature.

Programme planning

The teacher must know what is to be achieved and programme accordingly so that all the conditions for learning, as set out on pages 4 and 5, are incorporated. Consider the following when planning to develop the children's knowledge about writing forms.

- Plan topics in advance so that resources can be collected and examples of particular writing forms can be built up.
- Think about the particular topic to be studied and the unique uses of language within that topic or subject area and plan modelling sessions to develop these.
- Programme so that modelling becomes a systematic and purpose-ful part of language sessions.
- Plan for writing activities across the curriculum and ensure that written activities for the subject or content areas are not limited to one word or one sentence responses.
- Use published texts (books, extracts from books, newspaper articles etc.) as much as possible to demonstrate good writing forms. Examine these resources to see what teaching points can be gleaned from each one.
- Select those books that can be used for shared book experiences (big books or multiple copies of books) and plan sessions that

will focus on the writing models or teaching points you wish to develop.

● Ensure that the children use a range of writing forms and have a balance of writing across the curriculum and their own personal writing.

Figure 2.1: How language activities are drawn from the content areas of the curriculum

Content area	**e.g.** Environmental Studies
Topic	**e.g.** 'The Sea'
Understanding related to the topic	What you want the children to gain from the Unit of Work
Curriculum areas related to the topic	**e.g.** Maths, Science, Art, Health etc.
Language activities from the curriculum areas	**e.g.** Reading, Writing, Poetry, Oral Language etc.
Written language activities	**e.g.** Report writing, Narratives, Letters, Recounts, Opinions, Explanations etc.
Spelling focuses	**e.g.** The graphophonic, visual or morphemic knowledge that can be drawn from the written language activities, see Figure 2.2.

Figure 2.2: How specific spelling focuses can be drawn from a constructed text.

GRAPHOPHONIC
Discuss the ways the "sh" as in shed sound can be represented in words. List all suggested words.

MORPHEMIC
Discuss the use of the past tense using "d" or "ed."

MORPHEMIC
Finding the base words and then building new words from the base, e.g. differ, differing, difference, differently, etc.

MORPHEMIC
Discuss use of prefixes. List as many prefixes as possible.

Sharks are a very ancient group of animals which are thought to have lived in the seas for more than 300 million years. They have changed very little during that time. They are different to other fish and belong to the group called cartilaginous fish because, unlike most fish, they do not have any bones in their bodies. Their skeletons are made of cartilage. Skates and rays also belong to this group.

VISUAL
Discuss, list and study words with "ion" pattern

VISUAL
Listing words with "ous" pattern of words.

MORPHEMIC
Dictionary skills. Find meanings of selected words.

● Try to draw all language activities from the content areas of the curriculum.

● Decide how you plan to use the content area and the related resources to further the children's knowledge of writing forms. It could be done in one of the of the following ways:

▷ Select examples of the chosen writing form and use the similarities of purpose and form between these as the basis of the modelling experiences.

For example: read to the children a selection of reports

(perhaps on animals) and note the common types of information included in each report or note the common structure of
the reports.

   ▷ Select as many different writing forms on the topic being
studied and use these differences in form and purpose to start
the modelling experiences.

   For example: read a narrative and a factual text on a chosen
topic (perhaps about a particular animal) and note the way
the author has structured each text for a different purpose or
compare what the author would have needed to know to
write the respective texts.

- Plan to frequently read and share with the children as many as
possible of the selected books and writing forms.

- Allow time for the children to discuss these books and to
organise their knowledge about the writing forms presented.

- Plan for different approaches to reading and writing factual and
narrative texts. Remember factual and fiction books cannot
always be presented in the same manner as each other. Sections
of factual books can be read to the children, parts of the book
can be shared, emphasis could be on how the information is
organised etc. Often factual books do not need to be read in
their entirety (from cover to cover) to gain meaning from the
text. Fiction books need to be read in the correct sequence (even
if it is just skimming the text) to gain the author's meaning.

- Plan to write in front of the children in the chosen writing form
or jointly construct texts with them and use these opportunities
to develop their knowledge of the many purposes
and forms of written language. These activities can be done in
the Introductory or Model/Focus Period (see pages 14 and 15
for details) of language sessions or as an integral part of the
content area of the curriculum.

- Select from the content areas of the curriculum oral, written and
reading activities that will demonstrate the chosen writing form.

- Allow the children to explore and experiment with the writing
form in selected activities before expecting them to use this form
in their own writing.

- Formulate questions, related to writing form, to include in the
conference sessions with children on their own writing. For
example:

   ▷ What did you need to know to write this?

   ▷ What is the target audience for this writing?

   ▷ What is the purpose of this writing? (or) Why was this
written?

   ▷ How have you organised/presented the information?

- Check if the child is able to identify the form of writing used
and some of its unique characteristics.

- Provide an audience for the children's writing to give them an opportunity to reflect on and discuss their writing.
- Be aware that one piece of writing may have several forms of writing within it according to the purpose of each part.

Planning the language session

The teacher needs to provide opportunities for reading, writing and oral language activities and as these aspects of language are intertwined and interdependent the timetable would simply read Language Activities or Language. A large block of time should be allocated instead of fragmented smaller periods. The language session must include opportunities to demonstrate, explore, experiment with, share and practise all language skills. The following aspects would need to be planned for and included in most language sessions.

USSR (Uninterrupted, Sustained, Silent Reading)

USSR would include all participants (teachers as well as children) reading silently the books they have selected. These books may be from classroom displays, commercially produced books or constructed books.

Model or focus period

This may include the modelling, demonstration, drawing attention to or teaching of a particular aspect of reading, writing or oral language and generally involves the whole class but can involve small groups only.

Individual activity time

This may include compulsory or free choice individual reading, writing or oral language activities.

Share time

This is usually held at the end of a language session or at the end of one section of the language session. It may involve groups or the whole class and provides valuable teachable moments for the teacher as the children reflect upon and share each other's language work.

Conferences

These are the interactions between the teacher and child with regard to the child's work. They can be individual or small group conferences.

Clinics

These are based on the needs of individuals, groups or the whole class and involve the teacher's intervention in the child's learning process when the need arises. The clinics provide opportunities for the children to further develop their language skills and knowledge.

The following language session format is based on a two-hour period and suggests where the modelling of writing forms fits into the format.

It is not intended that the focus or model will be the same each week. For example the focus may be on a writing form one week, spelling, grammar or punctuation the next (or perhaps reading or oral language the next). Alternatively, the focus could change daily; for example, a writing form one day, a spelling focus the next, punctuation the next etc.

USSR . . . 15–20 minutes
This period may involve the children browsing, selecting and reading books from the classroom display that are based on the writing form being explored.

Model or Focus Period. . . 15 minutes
This period may include implicit or explicit modelling of the writing form being explored.

Exploration or Application Time . . . 15–20 minutes
This may involve individual, group or whole class reading, writing or oral activities related to the above focus or modelling period.

Share Time . . . 10 minutes
This may involve the sharing of individual, group, or class activities based on the focus or modelling period.

Model or Focus Time . . . 10 minutes
This may include implicit or explicit modelling of a particular language focus or may include instructions for and explanations of the work to follow.

Own Language Activities . . . 40 minutes
This may include free-choice language activities or compulsory activities that may be related to the focus or modelling period of the session.

Share Time . . . 5 minutes
This is an important time when the whole class is drawn together to discuss the reading, writing and oral language activities that have been attempted.

Planning for ways to help children explore the writing forms

It is important that the various writing forms are not only modelled but that the children have opportunities to further explore these forms and experiment with them before they become a part of their writing repertoire. The following are suggestions of ways of helping the children become familiar with using different writing forms.

Co-operative group work

Co-operative group work is a very positive way of helping children develop understanding of the purpose and structure of particular forms of writing and to enable them to experiment with a chosen form of writing within a supportive environment. They can refine their knowledge of a writing form through group discussion and demonstration and produce a piece of this form of writing as part of a team.

Through co-operative group work the teacher can ensure that each child has attempted the writing form and can evaluate the group's understanding of the form by observation of its members' work habits.

Arrange the children into groups (three children per group works well) and provide these groups with large sheets of butcher's paper and thick textas so that they can produce examples of the chosen writing form. The use of butcher's paper allows all group members to see and work on the writing task. Large sheets also enable the work to be easily seen by all class members during share time activities.

Use the Introductory or Model or Focus Period of language sessions to model, discuss and explore with the children the chosen writing form and then set the co-operative groups to work on their joint writing projects for about fifteen or twenty minutes (in the Exploration/Application Period) before going on with their own individual writing.

The lessons are conducted this way approximately four times a week. Often at the end of the week the co-operative groups have a final draft written which can be shared with all class members and used by the teacher for teaching or evaluation purposes. These final drafts of the writing form may be all that is required but some groups may wish to publish their work, in which case the time will need to be extended.

Class-books or big books to which each group has contributed can be completed this way or individual group books can be produced. These books can then be used as models for the children as they work on their own writing.

Co-operative groups may be given some of the following tasks which are related to writing forms:

♦ Writing on the same topic using the same writing form.
♦ Writing using the same form but different topics.
♦ Writing on the same topic but using any writing form.
♦ Free choice of topic and writing form.
♦ A problem involving a writing activity is presented and the groups work on it. For example, 'As a follow up to our excursion hand in a written presentation on the experience'. (This approach could also be used for oral, audio-visual and art presentations as well.)

Sometimes this procedure may go on for longer than a week depending on the task and the interest of the children. It is only one way of organising co-operative groups to work on modelled writing forms. It is not intended to be routinely used each week but could be used a couple of times in a term to help the children work with a new writing form. The approach can be modified to help children explore, experiment and practise other aspects of language.

Try it time

Another approach that will ensure the children experiment with and practise new writing forms that have been modelled is to allocate ten to fifteen minutes of the writing session to 'Try It Time'. During this time the children and the teacher individually write using a given writing form. This could be done in the Exploration or Application Period of the language session.

At the end of this time individuals may share their work with a partner, a small group or the whole class. This sharing time is valuable in helping children clarify the pertinent points in the structure of the writing form being modelled.

The use of contracts

Contract Writing can be another way of ensuring the children attempt a range of writing forms. This can be organised on a weekly, monthly or term basis and requires the children to negotiate the writing tasks to be completed in a given time (see Figure 2.3).

The same procedure could be used for Reading Contracts in which the children would be required to read a variety of books in varying writing forms (see Figure 2.4).

Figure 2.3: A student's writing contract

MY WRITING CONTRACT

NAME _Katherine C_   GRADE _6_

I _Katherine_ _____ agree to write the following

a report, my diary, and an advertisement for our school fete

by _30/5_   and present _the report_   in

published form.

SIGNED _K.C._

TEACHER'S SIGNATURE _L. Wing Jan_

DATE _29/4_

Figure 2.4: A student's reading contract

MY READING CONTRACT

NAME _Miki P._   GRADE _6_

I _Miki_ _____ agree to read the following

by _23/5_   and complete a book activity on _two_   of these.

NARRATIVE ✓   FACTUAL BOOK ✓   COMIC ✓
MAGAZINE ✓   JOKES AND RIDDLES BOOK   NEWSPAPER
BIOGRAPHY   POETRY COLLECTION

OTHER _Recipe Books_

SIGNED _M.P._

TEACHER'S SIGNATURE _L. Wing Jan_

DATE _30/4_

Record keeping, assessment and evaluation

Assessment and evaluation need to be an integral part of an ongoing process in any language programme. This does not imply that unrelated or contrived activities need to be devised to conduct evaluation. The following strategies can be used for effective evaluation.

Teacher's records

1 Observation of children's writing and reading behaviours

Decide what aspect of language you wish to study during any one session or period of time and use this as the focus of your observations. For example, you may wish to see who plans appropriately before actually writing, so you observe the children and note their behaviour and progress as revealed. This information can be recorded on check-lists or in anecdotal records.

2 Anecdotal records

These records can be compiled during a conference with a child or written as a reflection on a child's language development. These anecdotal records may consist of a single page for each child on which a dated entry is written as a result. (Figure 2.5)

Figure 2.5: Written language anecdotal records

NAME *Darren*			GRADE 6
Date	Stage	Topic/form	Comments
27/2	1st Draft	School Camp — Recount	Wrote events in sequence. Talked to him about use of pronouns.
15/3	1st Draft	Beach Cricket Procedural	Able to write clear instructions Needs to add headings for each section.

3 Collection and study of children's own writing

Samples of each child's drafts are collected, dated and filed away in individual writing files and periodically the teacher can refer to these and assess the writing development and knowledge of each child.

Figure 2.6: Student's evaluation sheet

MY WRITING SELF-EVALUATION FORM

NAME _Alischa_   DATE _6th June_

I can write a factual text. ☑

I can plan for factual writing. ☑

I know the difference between opinion and fact. ☐

I use diagrams, tables and graphs to represent some of the factual

information. ☐

I make sure the information I use is accurate. ☐

I have written   autobiography ☑   report ☐   explanation ☑

other ☑ : _an advertisement_

I have learnt to _make Did You Know Charts, Fact Trees and What I Need to Know Charts_

I can write a narrative text. ☑

I can plan for narrative writing. ☑

I can develop character profiles. ☑

I can write a word picture for the setting. ☑

I have written   poems ☐   jokes ☐   riddles ☐   stories ☑

other ☑ : _legend, limerick and cinquain_

I have learnt to _draw story maps and good endings to my storys_

Figure 2.7: Pupil self-evaluation sheet

WRITING SELF-EVALUATION—TERM _2_

NAME _Jodie_   DATE _June_

Things I have learnt: _That story writing is not the only style of writing. To make really good descriptions of a character and a setting. How to rewrite drafts._

I would like to: _get better with my publishing._

Student's records

The children must be a part of the evaluation and assessment strategy and the following records can be kept by them.

1 Pupil self-evaluation sheets

Periodically the children may be asked to reflect on and assess their own knowledge and use of writing forms. This can be done in the following ways:

i The child can complete an evaluation sheet formulated by the teacher to examine a particular aspect of his or her understanding of a writing form. (Figure 2.6)

ii The child may reflect on his or her writing and knowledge of writing forms and write a descriptive passage on his or her progress and needs. (Figure 2.7)

2 Writing records

As each child completes or files away a piece of writing which is no longer being worked on, whether it be a first draft or a published piece, an entry is made on his or her individual writing record. (Figure 2.8)

Figure 2.8: Student's writing record

MY WRITING RECORD	NAME Emma			
Title	Form	Draft	Pub.	Date
School Camp	Factual	✓		27/2
Water Cycle	Experiment	✓	✓	12/3
Autobiography	Factual	✓		26/3
The Space Monsters	Fiction	✓		29/4
Heart Facts	Factual	✓	✓	12/5

General evaluation of writing forms

A suggested summary of the general aspects of factual writing is given on page 28 and narrative writing on page 95. You may wish to use these for your own particular evaluation needs. They may also help you to set objectives for your written language programme. The formation of objectives and the consequent selection of evaluation checks will be dependent on the language development of the children being taught. For more specific aspects refer to the evaluation and assessment section included for each particular writing form; for example a summary of the general aspects of Recounts is given on page 82.

FACTUAL WRITING

▼

In this book the term 'factual text' is used to refer to those writing forms concerned with fact that have identifiable structures, stages and conventions and perform the function of informing the readers and enabling them to explore, question or challenge issues. Factual texts are functional forms of writing which have the purpose of enabling the reader and the writer to effectively participate in everyday life. Some forms of factual writing are:

- reports
- explanations
- procedures
- persuasive writing (either advertisement or argument)
- interviews
- surveys
- descriptions
- biographies
- recounts.

Narrative Information texts are included in this factual writing section because the narrative form is only used by the author as a method of conveying factual information.

It is important to note that sometimes a single piece of writing will include several different writing forms depending on the purpose of each section of the text.

To enable children to write factual texts with the same confidence that they use when writing narratives, they need opportunities to learn about the structure and function of factual texts. Some forms of factual writing (for example, explanations, persuasive writing) are rarely written by children in primary school so they need to be exposed to the implicit and explicit modelling of these forms.

A balanced writing program would include a focus on factual writing as well as fiction writing.

It is the teacher's role to provide a writing programme that includes a focus on factual writing as well as on narrative writing. This focus can be introduced in the early years of primary school and developed more extensively as the child progresses through the school. Factual writing can be an authentic activity if introduced through a programme that plans for writing across the curriculum. (See Chapter 2 for suggestions for programme planning.)

The success of the factual writing programme can be judged when the children start to use writing forms appropriate to the purposes and audience of the writing and when the common characteristics of a writing form are not only recognised by the children but are used in their own writing.

General activities with factual texts

The following activities are designed to help children become familiar with the language of factual texts and to develop the skills of reading, interpreting and writing these texts. Each activity can be adapted by teachers to suit their class and programme needs. Some of these activities can also be used with narrative texts.

1 Prediction activities

From the cover, title or blurb of a book or from flicking through it the children can predict:
- the subject
- the writing form used

- the organisation of the information within the book
- the terms used
- the intended audience for the book.

2 'What I Know About . . .' charts

The children write these charts before and after reading factual texts. They compare the results of both. This can be an individual, group or class activity. For example, before reading a book about turtles, the children write down all they *know* about the subject. When they have finished reading the book they compile a list of what they *learnt* about turtles. This helps them to focus on the content of the book.

3 'Did You Know?'

The children compile information in question format after reading factual texts. For example, when the children have finished reading a factual text they write down the facts they gained in the form of questions to stimulate the reader's interest. This activity is a good way of assessing the children's understanding of the content of the text.

4 'What the Author Needed to Know' activities

The children list what the author needed to know to be able to write the book. These lists can be compiled before and/or after reading and can be used with factual texts or fiction books. For example, the children read:

i   A factual text and then list what facts the author needed to know to write the text.

ii A fiction book and then list any factual information the author needed to know before writing the book.

iii A factual and a fiction book about the same topic and compare the type of information each author needed before writing the respective book.

iv Two or more factual books on the same topic and compare the information each author needed to write each book.

The above activities are useful ways of checking the children's comprehension skills as well as their knowledge of the work of authors.

5 Information sorting

For example:

i   Written statements based on a text that the children have read can be sorted into true/false or fact/opinion categories.

ii Information can be sorted into given headings. For example, information about 'Lions' could be sorted into the following categories: Food, Enemies, The Young, Habitat etc.

6 'Fact trees'

The children are required to read a text and write concise facts based on the information gained from it. They may write these facts as branches of a tree with the trunk being the subject of the activity. When all the facts have been added the children sequence these into the order they wish to write them in their own factual text. See page 32.

7 Write, read, write activities

For example:
i   The text is covered so that only the illustrations remain. The children study the illustrations and write their own text. The text is uncovered and read by the children who then rewrite their own information to include any extra information they may have gained.
ii As for (i) but the children write questions about the illustrations and after reading the text check if their questions were answered.

8 Text analysis

These activities are designed to focus on the structure of different texts and they also help with assessing the comprehension skills of the child. For example:
i   The children read a text and add headings that will be appropriate for the content of each paragraph or section.
ii The children read a text and explain why the information is grouped as it is.

9 Writing to headings

The children are provided with a series of headings related to a topic being studied and they are required to write information for each heading. For example: the headings Description, Food, Enemies, Habitat, Movement etc. may be provided for a report on an animal and the children research and write information for these headings.

10 Jumbled information

For example:
i   Sentences based on a subject are written on separate pieces of card. The children read the sentences, regroup them appropriately according to the content of each card and add suitable

headings for each group of sentences. If the topic was about a country, for example, there would be a series of sentences for each of the following aspects: Population, Climate, Location, Description etc. Each sentence would be written on a separate card and the children would group the related sentences.

ii Separate paragraphs on different aspects of a given topic can be written on the cards and then the children proceed as above.

11 Labelling activities

For example:

i   After reading a text the children must draw a diagram to represent the information and provide suitable labels.

ii The teacher provides an unlabelled diagram and the children, after reading the text, provide the labels.

12 Retelling procedures

For example:

i   The teacher reads a factual text and the children orally retell the content.

ii   As above but the children **write** a retelling.

iii The **children** read a factual text and orally retell it.

iv   As above but the children **write** the retelling.

v   The children and teacher share a factual text (perhaps during a shared book experience) and jointly construct a written retelling.

13 'Ask the Expert' sessions

These can be individual or group activities. The children select a topic of their own choice, research it and prepare an oral presentation to the class. For example, a child may choose to research how a bicycle pump works. When the research is completed the child prepares and presents this information to the class in the form of an oral activity. The remainder of the grade can ask questions at the conclusion of the presentation. This activity is a good way of introducing children to skills required for writing a factual text (research skills, note-taking skills, organising the information etc.).

14 Readers' circle

This activity can involve the whole class in one large circle or may consist of several small groups with an interested adult leading the discussion. For example:

i   The children bring to the circle a factual book they have read and take the opportunity to share and compare the various forms of factual writing.

Readers' Circle enables children to share and compare various writing forms.

ii The teacher may set a contract in which the whole class or a small group is required to read a factual text and prepare for a Readers' Circle at a later date.

15 Authors' circle

This activity is conducted as above but the children have an opportunity to share their own attempts at factual writing and gain valuable feedback from an audience.

16 Partner reading/writing activities

For example:
i One partner writes questions about a topic for the other partner to research and write answers in an appropriate form.
ii One partner reads a text and retells this to the other.
iii The partners jointly write a factual text to present to the class.
iv The children share the reading of a factual text and present the information in chart or poster form.

'Beat the Panel' activities encourage the reading of factual texts.

17 'Beat the Panel' activities

For example:
i A panel of three children is given a topic (usually drawn from a subject being studied in class) and they must research it until they think they are well prepared. They present an oral report to the class and attempt to answer questions put by the children.
ii An alternative to this is to give the panel information to read and prepare for question time by the class, who have also read the information. The panel starts with twenty points. Each

time a panel member can't answer a question the panel loses five points. A correct answer gains five points. After a set number of questions the score is recorded. Another panel is formed to repeat the procedure on another topic at a later date. Each group's score is kept to see which one is the champion panel.

iii Another approach is to have each panel member read the information and prepare for a competition against the other panel members. The class also reads the information and asks the panel questions related to the text. The first panel member to answer correctly scores a point. The member with the most points at the end of a given number of questions wins the game.

18 Changing form

The children present given information in a different writing form. For example:

i A recipe may be presented as a series of diagrams.

ii A diagram of the water cycle may be presented as an explanation.

iii An explanation of how milk is pastuerised may be presented as a set of instructions.

Assessment and evaluation of factual writing

This is a suggested summary of aspects you may wish to use for your own particular evaluation needs. They may help you to set specific objectives for this aspect of your language programme. The selection of objectives will be dependent on the language development of the children you teach.

- Able to explain the difference between factual and narrative texts.
- Able to explain the function of different forms of factual writing.
- Able to plan for factual writing (guiding questions, note-taking etc.).
- Attempts some factual writing in independent/free choice writing activities.
- Understands the importance of accurate information in factual texts.
- Able to use diagrams, tables, graphs and other graphic forms to present information.
- Able to distinguish between fact and opinion.

REPORTS

Description

Reports are used to present factual information in a concise, accurate manner without any irrelevant details. They contain a logical sequence of facts that are stated without any personal involvement or bias from the author. For example: 'The policeman signalled for the driver to pull over to the curb. He produced his notebook and proceeded to book the driver for failing to stop at the school crossing.'

Reports can be all-encompassing and can include generalisations about the subject matter. They focus on classes or groups of things. For example: 'Koalas are Australian marsupials. They eat leaves from the eucalypt trees and have very sharp claws to enable them to climb the trees to reach these leaves.'

Learning experiences for reports

- Discuss the point that most reports begin with a general classification of the subject matter and then proceed onto descriptive writing which is organised into interrelated sections. For example:

General classification ———→ Elephants are mammals. They are the largest living land animals. There are two species, the African and the Indian.

Description written in related groups of information ———→ The main differences between the two species are the larger ears and tusks of the African and the two lips at the end of its trunk compared to the one lip at the end of the Indian elephant's trunk.

The African elephant is found in most parts of Africa and can
live in semi-desert, bush, forest, the savannah and river valleys. The
Indian elephant can be found in Sri Lanka, Burma, Thailand and
Malaysia.

Both species move in groups called herds comprising of cows,
bulls and calves and each of these herds is led by an older cow.
The older males (bulls) only join the herd to mate.

Description written in related groups of information

- Use this organisation of interrelated information to demonstrate paragraphing to children and guide them toward using this writing convention in their own reports.
- Discuss the use of the language in reports.
  ▷ Note that most reports use very economical speech.
  ▷ The language is not flowery and does not employ unnecessary descriptive devices, for example irrelevant adjectives, adverbs, similes, metaphors etc.
  ▷ The use of personal pronouns is limited as reports aren't written in a personal manner.
  ▷ Most reports are written in the present tense.
  ▷ Some reports use technical or scientific terms in the information.
- Discuss the point that reports deal with facts so therefore the information must be as accurate as possible.
- Demonstrate and discuss the various procedures for checking the reliability of information presented in the children's reports. For example:
  ▷ Reading several sources of information to confirm common statements or generalisations.
  ▷ If the report is based on information gained from interviews it may be necessary to review the report with the interviewee or even to confirm the information by conducting a further interview, if possible, with another appropriate person.
- Model the use of acknowledgements, bibliographies, reference lists and the citing of references etc. in your own or jointly constructed texts and encourage the children to use these in their own writing.
- Use modelling (either your own writing or a jointly constructed text) to demonstrate how to plan for report writing. For example:
  ▷ Emphasise the importance of knowing what you wish to write about. It is useful to make a plan of the information to be included in the report by asking the children 'What would you like included in a text about . . .?'. The children are asked to suggest headings rather than sentences for the type of information they would like to see included. These headings

Figure 4.1: 'What I Want to Write About . . .' chart

What I Want to Write About Dolphins
Description
Enemies
Habitat
Breeding
Food
Movement
Communication

Figure 4.2: 'What I Know About . . .' chart

What I Know About Dolphins
◆ Live in the sea
◆ Live in large groups called schools
◆ Are very intelligent
◆ Are mammals
◆ Get caught in driftnets
◆ Have a nostril on the top of the head

Figure 4.4: Research Guide Chart

My Research Guide
I can get help from . . .
◆ The school library
◆ The local library
◆ John's Dad
◆ Encyclopedias
◆ The Marine Centre
◆ The Zoo
◆ The Aquarium

are written on a 'What I Want to Write About Chart' (Figure 4.1).

▷ Encourage the children to explore their previous knowledge of the subject. To help the children narrow down their research work have them use headings to form 'What I Know About . . .' charts based on their current knowledge of the topic (Figure 4.2).

▷ Help the children formulate efficient research tasks. The information in the above charts indicates the areas in which information is required and this provides a framework for the formation of guiding questions necessary for purposeful research. These questions can be written on a 'What I Need to Know' chart (Figure 4.3).

▷ Demonstrate how to plan for the location of the required information. Compile a list of possible sources of information to emphasise the range of research that can be undertaken. This can be referred to as a Research Guide Chart (Figure 4.4).

▷ Help the children develop effective note-taking skills. Demonstrate how to read for specific information and how to write brief notes from this reading. The construction of 'Fact Trees' (Figure 4.5, page 32) while reading for information is an effective way of helping children develop note-taking skills.

Figure 4.3: 'What I Need to Know About' chart

What I Need To Know About Dolphins
FOOD
What do they eat?
How do they catch it?
How much do they eat daily?
HABITAT
Where are they found?
Why?
Are they migratory?
DESCRIPTION
How many species of dolphin are there?
What is the average size of an adult dolphin?
How small is a new born dolphin?

This chart gives the children guidance for their reading and note-taking.
After referring to the 'What I Want To Write About' chart and the 'What I Know About' chart the children compile a list of questions to guide their research for the information they still require. They can place a tick beside the questions as they find the answers to them.

Activities for report writing

Many of these activities can be adapted to be used as oral, written or reading activities. The same thing applies to the actual organisation of the activities as they can be altered for use by small groups, individuals or the whole class. Further activities can be found in the section entitled 'General Activities With Factual Texts'.

Specific information on the modelling procedure can be found in the 'Organisation, Planning and Management' section. The following activities are designed to further integrate and develop the children's understanding of the purpose, structure and language of reports.

Figure 4.5: Fact Trees

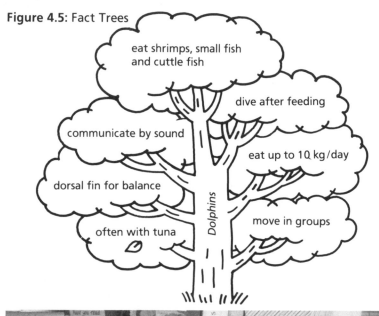

Partner reading activities help the children understand the structure of factual texts.

1 Find the facts

Read a factual text to the children and they must write down two or three of the important facts. Order these according to the children's ideas of importance.

2 Text titles

Use an overhead projector to display a short report. Ask the children to provide a heading for the text after reading its content.

3 Text analysis

Use the text as above but ask the children to suggest what each part of the text is about. This will enable them to see how the text is constructed.

4 Ask the expert

The children prepare an oral report to be presented to the class on a topic of their choice. They must be prepared to answer questions about their chosen topic so they may need to read up on it. This is a meaningful way of encouraging the children to read for information.

5 Beat the panel

For general details of this activity refer to the 'General Activities with Factual Texts' section.

A group of children (three to four children works well) is given a report to read on a chosen subject. It is desirable that the topic is related to the work being studied in the classroom. The group is given a nominated time to read the report and to become 'experts' on the subject. At the same time the remainder of the class is required to read the same article and compose questions to ask 'The Experts' about the article. The panel gains points for each correct answer and the class gains points for those questions related to the article that the panel cannot answer. This activity both encourages the reading of factual texts and develops the ability to recognise important facts in a report.

6 News reports

Individuals or a small group of children are given the task of presenting a report on the week's news. Emphasis is on reporting the facts and not opinion.

7 Racy reports

Children are asked to report, for example, on a class or school news event in a set time frame; one minute for instance. Only the most important facts can be stated. This helps to develop the ability to select the most relevant and appropriate facts.

8 Reports in brief

This is a written adaptation of Racy Reports. The children must write a report on a nominated topic, or one of their own choice, using a given number of words or in a given time limit. For example:
- Write about lions in fifty words — no more, no less.
- In five minutes only, write all you know about lions.
- Write a paragraph or four sentences about the lions' habitat.

9 Write, read, write

The children are given a picture from a report, or a copy of a report with the text masked and only the pictures, diagrams and/or title visible. They write their own report for the pictures and share these with partners. The original text is uncovered and read by the children who then rewrite their reports to include the facts in the original text.

10 Writing to headings

The children can compose their own reports using guiding headings. This is a very good way to help the children organise their information for reports. For example:
- If the children are writing about a class topic on animals the headings may be: Description, Habitat, Food, Enemies, etc.

11 Partner reading/writing activities

The children can read reports to each other and recall the important facts or they can write a jointly constructed report on a topic they have read about. This activity helps them understand and use the structure for report writing.

12 Grouping information

For example:
- Provide the children with a series of facts related to a particular topic. The children must group related facts ready for writing.
- The children brainstorm all the information related to a set topic and then group this information into related facts. They may then provide a heading for each of these groups of information.

These grouping activities help the children develop a structure for report writing.

Assessment and evaluation for report writing

This is a suggested summary of aspects you may wish to use for your own particular evaluation needs. They may help you to set specific objectives for this aspect of your language programme. The selection of objectives will be dependent on the language development of the children you teach. The student is able to:

- understand the purpose of reports.
- use report writing appropriately.
- identify/read/write reports.
- plan for report writing.
- take take brief notes.
- identify/write generalisations.
- identify/write descriptive information.
- organise facts in logical sequence.
- write reports with sense of unity.
- write to guiding headings.
- state facts without bias or opinion.
- support facts with relevant details.
- identify trivial/irrelevant facts.
- use language appropriate to reports.
- cite sources of information.

Exploring reports with the children— a sample unit

This sample unit includes ideas for modelling sessions to be used within a language lesson. The modelling time would take no more than fifteen to twenty minutes. The suggestions for further activities would take extra time and may or may not be added to the modelling session time. They may be conducted in separate sessions with individual children, groups or the whole class.

Demonstration book:

Five Trees by Jim Howes (Southern Cross Series, Macmillan, 1987) also available in big book format.

Session One

> **Focus**—How writers plan for report writing

- Show the children the cover only of *Five Trees*. Do not show them inside the book.
- Predict and discuss:
  ▷ What type of book do you expect this to be?
  ▷ What do you think is meant by the title?
- Ask them to write, discuss and brainstorm what headings for information about trees they would need to include in a book about this subject. List these on a 'What We Need to Write About Trees' chart. For example, Types of Trees, What Trees Need to Grow, Importance of Trees etc.
- The children then brainstorm what they already know about trees under each of the listed headings. This could be compiled on a 'What We Know About Trees' chart.
- Read and share with the children the section 'Why Trees?'

Further activities

- As the children discover further information about trees it is added to the charts formed in the above session. For example:
  ▷ They may wish to add further headings to the 'What We Need to Write About Trees' chart.
  ▷ They may add further facts to the 'What We Know About Trees' chart.
- Set up a display of books about trees (both factual and fiction books) and allow the children to browse, select and read.
- Share some of these books with the children and discuss the different information each author would have needed to write his or her book.

Session Two

> **Focus**—How introductory passages are written

- Look at the Table of Contents in *Five Trees* and try to work out the name of each tree described by each chapter heading.
- The children confirm or alter their predictions by turning to each section in turn and sharing the introductory passage only. Keep the remainder of the text covered.
- Discuss the purpose and style of these introductory passages.
- Model write an introductory passage for another tree, or for a plant, a bird or an animal, on which a report could be written.

Further activities

- Jointly construct introductory passages for any subject as opportunities arise.
- Take every opportunity to read, note, model and discuss introductions in both fiction and factual books.
- Find samples of introductions to reports and use these for demonstration purposes, cloze activities, prediction activities etc.

Session Three

> **Focus** — Forming guiding questions for research

- Select one of the trees from the book and ask the children to list all the questions they would like answered about that tree. Compile all these questions onto a 'What We Want to Know About Trees' chart. This can be done by:
  - ▷ Reading together one of the chapters on one of the trees and ticking off the questions as they are answered in the text. *Do not read to or show the children the double-page spread on each of the trees as these are to be used in a later session.* The above outlined procedure could be repeated for each of the trees, in subsequent modelling sessions.
  - ▷ Alternatively, divide the children into groups, with each group having the name of one of the five trees in the book. Each group must compile questions they would like answered about their particular tree. These are recorded as for the above activity. As each chapter is read in a shared book session the children tick off the answered questions. Note: if this latter procedure is adopted more or longer shared book sessions will need to be planned to cover all the work.

Further activities

- Set research tasks to find the answers to those questions listed that were not answered in *Five Trees*.
- The children select a plant or tree of their own choice and plan for writing by using 'What I Want to Write About', 'What I Know' and 'What I Need to Know' charts. This can be done individually or in groups.
- The children may keep adding to any class charts formed during this Unit of Work.

Session Four

> **Focus** — The use of diagrams in report writing

- Read with the children the section entitled 'A barrel-full of Good Ideas' on pages 6 and 7 of the book. Discuss the following:
  - ▷ What is distinctive or unusual about the format?
  - ▷ Why has the author presented the information in this format?
  - ▷ What headings are used on the page?
  - ▷ What sort of information lends itself to this type of format?
  - ▷ What device has been used to explain more clearly some of the text under the headings? (The focus drawings in the circles.)

  Any information gained from these pages can be added to the charts made in previous sessions.
- Predict what the double-page spread for the mangrove tree would include and then share this section with the children.

Further activities

- Select one or all of the remaining trees and ask the children to design their own double-page spread for the tree. Compare these with the book.
- Model the planning of a double-page spread that uses the devices in *Five Trees*.
- Jointly construct a double-page spread for a class book.
- Find other examples of the use of the strategies used in the book.
- Provide the children with a copy of the text from one of the double-page spreads and ask the children to format it as they think it should be on a double page.
- Provide the children with the name of and headings for information on a tree not included in the book. They write to the headings and provide related illustrations.
- The children may design their own double-page spread on any topic of their choice.
- Provide the children with a copy of text on any subject. They must pick out the information suitable for a double-page spread and then construct the page.

Session Five

> **Focus**—What the author needed to know to write the book

- Ask the children what the author needed to know to write this book. For example:
  - ▷ Refer to the Table of Contents and ask the children what he needed to know to write each chapter.
  - ▷ Turn to the Index and select some of the words listed and ask the children why these were included in the book. Refer to the pages indicated in the Index and reread information to help the children gain an idea of the enormity of the research the author must have done to write the book.

Further activities

- Model report writing on any topic.
- Read other reports to the children and compile with the children 'Did You Know?' Charts. (See page 24 for details of this procedure.)
- Each child or group selects one of the words in the Index and within a short time-limit researches it so that a new fact about the subject can be presented to the class.
- Groups reread a chapter and write a detailed account of what the author would have needed to know to write the chapter.

Books to further explore reports with the children

BB This indicates that a book is also available in big book format.

Bender, Lionel. *Kangaroos and Other Marsupials*. Gloucester Press, 1988.

Bolton, Faye & Cullen, Esther. *Animal Shelters*. Bookshelf, Martin Educational, 1987. **BB**

Cullen, Esther. *An Introduction To Australian Spiders*. Bookshelf, Martin Educational, 1986. **BB**

Croser, Josephine. *The Life of a Duck*. Magic Bean In-Fact Series, Era Publications, 1989. **BB**

Drew, David. *Caterpillar Diary*. Nelson, 1987. **BB**

Drew, David. *Mystery Monsters*. Nelson, 1988. **BB**

Drew, David. *Small Worlds*. Nelson, 1989. **BB**

Drew, David. *Gas Giants*. Nelson, 1989. **BB**

Green, Robyn. *Caterpillars*. Bookshelf, Martin Educational, 1986. **BB**

Howes, Jim. *Animal Jigsaws*. Southern Cross Series, Macmillan, 1987.

Howes, Jim. *Skin, Scales, Feather and Fur*. Southern Cross Series, Macmillan, 1987.

Lane, Margaret. *The Beaver*. Fontana Picture Lions. Collins, 1984.

Latham, Ross & Sloan, Peter. *Great Dinosaurs*. Harcourt Brace Jovanovich, 1989.

Morris, Jill. *Numbat Run*. Harcourt Brace Jovanovich, 1989. **BB**

Norman, David & Milner, Angela. *Dinosaur—Collins Eye Witness Guides*. Collins, 1989.

Pigdon, K. & Woolley, M. *Earthworms*. Southern Cross Series, Macmillan, 1989. **BB**

Ridpath, Ian. *The Giant Book of Space*. Hamlyn, 1989. **BB**

Short, Joan & Bird, Bettina. *Crocodilians*. Bookshelf, Martin Educational, 1988.

Sloan, P. & Latham, R. *Animal Reports*. Harcourt Brace Jovanovich, 1989. **BB**

Tyler, Michael. *An Introduction To Frogs*. Bookshelf Series, Ashton Scholastic, 1987.

Vaughn, Marcia. *Ships and Boats and Things That Float*. Harcourt Brace Jovanovich, 1989. **BB**

5

PROCEDURAL TEXTS

▼

Description

Procedural texts are used to either direct behaviour or to describe how something is done. They are often referred to as 'How To' texts as they include instructions. The information is presented in a logical sequence of events which is broken up into small steps. These texts are usually written in the present tense and in general terms to enable any person to use them. There is little use of personal pronouns.

Learning experiences for procedural texts

- There are different types of procedural texts for different purposes. Discuss this with the children. For example:
  - ▷ Texts that explain how something works or how it is used (instruction manuals, operations instructions).
  - ▷ Texts that instruct how to do a particular activity (recipes, science experiments, rules for games, stage directions, road safety rules etc.).
  - ▷ Texts that deal with human behaviour (essays on how to succeed, how to live happily, how to conduct a lifestyle etc.).
- Note that each type of procedural text has a standard format according to the purpose of the text. For example:
  - ▷ Recipes usually have the information presented in at least two basic groups: ingredients and method.

- ▷ Games instructions usually include instructions on how to play, rules of the game, method of scoring and the number of players.
- ▷ Scientific experiments usually include the purpose of the experiment, equipment, procedure, observations and conclusion.
- • Discuss the need to:
  - ▷ write so the instructions are clear (without any ambiguities)
  - ▷ make sure they are logical and easy to follow
  - ▷ trial or test the instructions with a representative of the target audience to ensure that the instructions are absolutely clear to the reader
  - ▷ rework instructions until they are 'foolproof'.
- • Formulate and use guiding questions to help the children clarify the purpose, audience and format of procedural texts that they may read or write. For example:
  - ▷ What is the text about?
  - ▷ What is the purpose of the text?
  - ▷ Who is the text written for?
  - ▷ Is the format appropriate for the subject of the procedural text?
  - ▷ Where did/will the author get the information?
- • Construct a variety of procedural texts in front of the children and ask them to identify the purpose and audience of each.
- • Use authentic, relevant situations to demonstrate the writing of procedural texts. For example:
  - ▷ Classroom routines could be jointly written by the children and the teacher for the purpose of instructing class members how to do tasks around the room and to explain how particular equipment in the classroom operates.
  - ▷ As a particular skill from any subject is taught, a chart or booklet can be written to remind the children of the process.
  - ▷ Classroom rules can be written and displayed around the room.
  - ▷ Use the content areas of the curriculum to draw out examples of procedural texts. For example: Science experiments; Health/first aid procedures; Keeping classroom pets; Maths activity-centre instructions etc.; Art/craft procedures or patterns; Phys. Ed. games, instructions and rules.
- • Discuss the vocabulary used in procedural texts. For example:
  - ▷ it varies according to the target audience
  - ▷ the more familiar the audience is with the topic the more technical terms are used in the text
  - ▷ list the technical terms used in the texts
  - ▷ list the vocabulary that is used to denote the time or sequence of events, for example before, after, then, while etc.
- • Ensure the children are aware of the target audience for their writing and provide these guiding questions for their consideration:

Classroom rules demonstrate a particular purpose and form of written language.

- ▷ Who is going to use the instructions?
- ▷ Can technical terms be used?
- ▷ Can bigger chunks of the process be written at the one time or does it need to be divided up into very small steps?

- Provide plenty of oral activities to develop the children's skill in sequencing events in small steps before expecting them to write instructions.
- Stress that procedural texts are written in general terms to enable anyone to execute the process being explained. Personal experiences are not written in this form.
- Note that often the instructions begin with a verb. For example: 'Pour the milk into the pan. Boil the milk. Mix the milk into the batter etc.' The discussion of the use of verbs in the texts can lead on to the use of adverbs and this is a very purposeful and relevant way of introducing the children to some aspects of grammar. For example the children may be asked to provide appropriate adverbs in a familiar recipe: 'Pour . . ., Mix . . ., etc.'
- Demonstrate how to write up classroom experiments in a standard format. Discuss why it is important to write according to this format every time an experiment is recorded.
- Read and discuss the format of recipes in particular books. Note that each recipe book may have a different format for recipes but within any one book these are set out in the same way. Discuss why this is the case.
- Compare the set out of a range of instruction manuals, games instructions or rules books and discuss the features of each.
- Note how diagrams, labels, tables, photographs, illustrations etc. are used to clarify instructions.

Activities for procedural texts

Many of these activities can be adapted to be used as oral, written or reading activities. The same applies to the actual organisation of the activities as they can be altered for use by small groups, individuals or the whole class. Further activities can be found in the 'General Activities With Factual Texts' section.

Specific information on the modelling procedure can be found in the 'Organisation, Planning and Management' section. The following activities are designed to further integrate and develop the children's understanding of procedural writing.

1 Group sort

As a group or a class activity collect examples of instructions from magazines etc. Group these according to given criteria and discuss the reasons for the given classification. For example:

- examples of 'good' or 'bad' instructions
- instructions related to technical topics and those related to human phenomena.
- examples of instructions that explain a procedure and those that direct a process.

2 Jumbled instructions

Give the children a set of jumbled instructions. They must arrange them in a logical sequence.

3 Finish the instructions

The children are given a sequence of instructions for a common task, for example making a phone call. The last steps are omitted and the children are required to write them in the same style.

4 Instruction cloze

Selected words are omitted from the instructions for a familiar task. The children are required to supply the appropriate words.

5 Heading cloze

The children are given a copy of a procedural text (recipe, experiment, game instructions etc.) and are required to provide the omitted headings.

6 Match up

Provide the children with a set of instructions and accompanying diagrams. They must match each instruction to the appropriate diagram.

7 Map mates

Provide a simple map (of the classroom, school, or local area, or it may be a map of an imaginary area) and the children must write the instructions on how to get from point A to point B. Share these and discuss the features of the 'best' instructions.

8 Oral wonder works

The children bring an object from home and explain how to use it.

9 Written wonder works

The same procedure as above but the children must draw and label the object and then write instructions for its use.

10 The expert—oral

The children must show an item they have made and then explain how it was made.

11 The expert—written

The children must write instructions to explain how they made a particular item.

12 Reporting on the expert

Someone performs a specific procedure, for example making something, cooking, playing a game etc. The children observe the procedure and are required to write it out in the most appropriate form.

13 Game making

The children make a board game (or any other type of game) and write the accompanying instructions. Headings can be given to help with the writing of the rules. For example:
- number of players
- the equipment required
- how to start
- how to finish
- the scoring of the game.

These games can be trialled in the classroom and instructions altered if necessary.

14 User-friendly instructions

The children can be divided into two groups and asked to write a set of instructions for the same activity but each group has a different 'Target Audience'. For example:
- 'How to order a lunch from the canteen' could be written as instructions for grade six children as well as for the parents.
- 'How to use the photocopier' could be written for a child and for a teacher etc.

Note that the topic chosen needs to be one with which the children are familiar.

15 Giving directions

The children conduct these activities in pairs. For example:
- Both children are given identical sets of coloured shapes. One child makes a pattern with one set of shapes and the other child (who has not seen the pattern) must replicate it following the verbal or written instructions of the partner.

- Both children are given unmarked grid paper. One child draws objects in several of the squares out of the view of the partner. The partner must replicate on the unmarked grid paper the position of the objects following verbal or written instructions.
- Each child is given two copies of the same map (real or imaginary). Each child marks in his or her own special features on one of their maps, for example school, park, office, pirate treasure, cave etc. On a separate piece of paper they write instructions on how to locate and draw in these places on the second unaltered map. The children swap the set of instructions and try to mark in the nominated places following the written instructions. The original maps the children made are used as checks on the accuracy of the instructions and the correctness of the reader's interpretation of the instructions.

Assessment and evaluation of procedural writing

This is a suggested summary of aspects you may wish to use for your own particular evaluation needs. They may help you to set specific objectives for this aspect of your language programme. The formation of objectives and the consequent selection of evaluation checks will be dependent on the language development of the children being taught. The student is able to:
- understand the purpose of procedural texts.
- recognise the different types of procedural texts.
- follow written directions or instructions.
- identify/read/write a variety of procedural texts.
- break down processes into a sequence of logical events.
- write directions in clear, precise language.
- use visual representation to clarify written directions.
- set up a trial situation and observe the implementation of written instructions.
- analyse faults in directions or instructions and rectify these.
- recognise technical terms in given procedural texts.

Exploring procedural texts— a sample unit

This sample unit includes ideas for modelling sessions to be used within a language lesson. The modelling time would take no more than fifteen to twenty minutes. The suggestions for further activities would take extra time and may or may not be added to the modelling session time. They may be conducted in separate sessions with individual children, groups or the whole class.

Demonstration book:

Kids in the Kitchen by Vikki Leng and Judith Ryles (Oxford University Press, 1989).

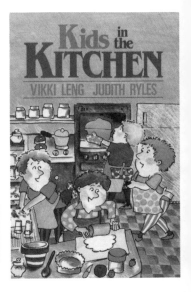

Session One

> **Focus**—Introduction to book: the format and organisation of information in one type of procedural text

- Show only the front cover of the book to the children who then make predictions about the contents of the book. They are to consider the following:
  ▷ What will the book be about? Why do you think this?
  ▷ What type of book will it be?
  ▷ What writing form will be used?
  ▷ What would you expect to find in this book?
  ▷ How would you expect the information to be arranged?
- Quickly flick through the pages of the book to allow the children to confirm or alter their predictions.
- Once the type of book and writing form have been established, close the book again and have the children write their predictions of some of the headings and/or vocabulary that would be used in the book. This activity can be done by brainstorming as a whole class or with the children working individually, or in pairs.
- Share these headings/vocabulary with the class and discuss why these may be used.
- Read the book with the children. As you read the children may tick off the headings/vocabulary they listed.
       You may not wish to read all the book in order but, rather, in sections to allow the children to get an overview of the book. Allow time for discussion as the children make discoveries about the book.

Further activities

- Have the children bring recipe books from home (both published books and family recipe books), collect a selection from the library, find recipes in magazines etc. and set up a display of these and allow the children time to browse, read and discuss the features of each.
- The children bring a copy of their favourite recipe and share this with the grade, partner etc.

Session Two

Focus — Cause and effect: procedural text in the form of rules

- Share with the children the section 'Tips For Safety' and discuss the following:
  - ▷ Do all recipe books have this section?
  - ▷ Why does this book have this section?
  - ▷ Why don't the hints end with full stops?
  - ▷ How are these hints written?
  - ▷ What is the difference between a rule and a hint?
- Note that each tip is written to suggest appropriate behaviour. Discuss why each tip does not state the reason for the suggested behaviour.
- Discuss the effect if each of these hints were not adhered to.
- Talk about cause and effect and the children can form reasons to add to each hint.
  The above activities could be used for the 'Hygiene Rules' section as well.

Further activities

- Model the writing of hints and the reasons. Share these with the class and display these.
- The children may write further safety hints related to cooking, school or classroom activities, road safety, water safety etc. but they are to include the reason for the hint.

Session Three

Focus — Procedural text in the form of instructions for cooking

- Select a couple of the recipes to read to the children. Discuss the following:
  - ▷ What is the same/different about the organisation of information in each recipe?
  - ▷ What devices are used to help the reader?
- Look at the headings used in the recipes and note the differences in the form of information under each heading. Discuss the following:
  - ▷ Could abbreviations have been used in the ingredients section?
  - ▷ Did each heading need to have precise details?
- Look at the information under the heading 'Method' and discuss how these are written and set out. Locate and list all the verbs used.

Further activities

• Model write your favourite recipe.
• Provide the children with the headings 'Equipment' and 'Ingredients'. They refer to the text and locate and list as many words as possible for each heading.
• Make a class-book of the children's favourite recipes. The children write these in the modelled form.
• Make a class-book of 'Revolting Recipes' in which the ingredients and equipment are most unusual. Children must still write in appropriate format.

Session Four

Focus—The organisation of information in a procedural text of recipes

• Without referring to the book get children to suggest their favourite recipes. List these and then ask the children to work out a way of grouping similar recipes, for example desserts, lollies, snacks, meat, chicken, breakfast etc. Discuss the many ways recipes can be grouped.
• Read the recipes 'Marathon Muesli' and 'Special Fruity Yoghurt' and ask the children to provide a reason why they could be grouped together.
• Do the same with 'Power Packs' and 'Tucker In a Taco'.
• Turn to the Contents section of the book and discuss:
  ▷ How the recipes are grouped.
  ▷ The publishing device that was used to make each section easy to find.
  ▷ How information is arranged in the Contents.
  ▷ The difference between a contents page and an index.

Further activities

• Look at other recipe books and see how the recipes are grouped.
• Refer to the Contents page in *Kids in the Kitchen* and jointly construct an index for this book.
• Provide the children with copies of recipes and make a Table of Contents.

Session Five

Focus—Using diagrams to clarify directions

- Read 'Instant Pizzas' with the children. (You may wish to cook this recipe in this session. If so, plan for a longer session.) Discuss:
  - ▷ How could the information in the Method section have been much clearer?
  - ▷ Model the use of simple diagrams to show the sequence of tasks in this recipe.
  - ▷ Share other recipe books that use visual strategies to help explain a procedure.

Further activities

- Take every opportunity to model the use of graphics to help clarify written procedures.
- The children can select a recipe from a class-book and create a series of diagrams for it.

Books to further explore procedural texts with the children

BB This indicates that a book is also available in big book format.

Amery, Heather. *The Knowhow Book of Batteries and Magnets*. Usborne, 1975.

Anderson, Honey & Boland, Julia. *Keeping Small Animals*. Martin Educational/ Ashton Scholastic, 1988.

Croser, Josephine. *Keeping Silkworms*. Magic Bean In-Fact Series, Era Publications, 1989. **BB**

Klein, Robin. *Robin Klein's Crookbook*. Methuen, 1987.

Klein, Robin. *Penny Pollard's Guide to Modern Manners*. Oxford University Press, 1989.

Leng, Vikki & Ryles, Judith. *Kids In The Kitchen*. Oxford University Press. 1989. **BB**

Parker, Eleanor. *Fun With Food*. Harcourt Brace Jovanovich, 1990. **BB**

Richardson, Lesley. *Your Microwave Cookbook*. Ashton Scholastic, 1987.

Sydenham, Shirley. *Let's Cook*. Southern Cross Series, Macmillan, 1989. **BB**

Tofts, Hannah. *The Paint Book*. Ashton Scholastic, 1989.

Tuffin, Bruce. *Bike Care*. Southern Cross Series, Macmillan, 1987.

Vaughn, Marcia. *Wombat Stew Cookbook*. Ashton Scholastic, 1989.

Watts, Barry. *The Amazing Magic Book*. Angus & Robertson, 1989.

Wheeler, Tony. *Get to Know Plants*. Martin Educational/Ashton Scholastic, 1988.

6

EXPLANATIONS

▼

Description

Explanation writing involves the stating of reasons for the appearance of given phenomena. It involves the interpretation or justification of how or why things come about. Explanations state events in sequence and usually answer the questions beginning with 'why' or 'how' about a process rather than an object. For example:

HOW THE BLOOD MOVES AROUND THE HEART ⟵———————— *The process to be explained*

The heart is a muscle that pumps blood around the body. The stale

blood flows through the vena cava into the right atrium and when

the right atrium gets filled the stale blood enters the right ventricle   *Events in explanation written in sequence*

through a valve. It is then pumped to the lungs where it gets

oxygen put into it and then it goes back to the heart and enters

the left atrium and flows into the left ventricle through a valve. It's

pumped from the left ventricle through the aorta and around the

body where it takes nutrients and oxygen to the body's cells. ——— *Use of present tense*

Learning experiences for explanations

◆ Provide both published and constructed models of explanations as this form of writing is not usually part of primary school children's writing repertoire.

- Allow plenty of experience with oral explanations before expecting the children to write effectively in this form.
- Scan texts to find the parts that explain how or why about an event or action.
- Use the procedure outlined in the 'Reports' section of this book to help children plan for explanation writing.
- Model explanation writing in authentic language situations as they arise. For example, to explain situations at school:
  ▷ why certain behaviour is expected at school
  ▷ how school rules are formed.
- Model explanation writing as part of writing across the curriculum. For example:
  ▷ Health Activities—Why we must eat a balanced diet.
  ▷ Science—How clouds are formed.
  ▷ Social Education—The reasons why the United Nations Organisation was formed.
- Read both procedural texts and explanations to the children and give them the opportunity to discover the differences and similarities. For example:
  ▷ Both explanations and procedures include a sequence of events.
  ▷ Procedures usually don't state reasons for the events.
  ▷ Explanations involve the stating of reasons for an activity or process.
- Locate, list and discuss the words in explanations that:
  ▷ link cause and effect (because, so, consequently etc.)
  ▷ join two or more ideas. This could lead on to a discussion of the work of conjunctions.
- Provide the children with opportunities to discover that although explanation writing requires the research and stating of facts the reasons behind the facts are the most important element.
- Focus the children's attention on the need to add reasons when writing explanations.
- Use the content areas of the curriculum as sources for the above activities. Science will provide many opportunities to explore the cause and effect relationship and to draw out appropriate material for the above activities.
- Use the cause and effect strategy to check the children's comprehension of stories they have read or heard. For example:
  ▷ What caused Little Red Riding Hood to meet the wolf?
  ▷ What made the woodcutter rush to the grandmother's cottage?
- Use explanation writing to discover the children's understanding of work, to check their general knowledge and their comprehension of reading material. For example:
  ▷ How does an earthquake occur?
  ▷ Explain why the sun rises in the east.
  ▷ Why did the Once-ler give the little boy the truffula seed in Dr Seuss's *The Lorax*?

Activities for explanations

1 Add the effect

Give the children a cause and have them state the effect of that cause. For example:

- It didn't rain for many months so . . .
- There was a build up of pressure under the earth's surface which . . .
- The dinosaurs couldn't adapt to the changing climate so . . .
- The boy splashed in the puddle and . . .

2 Add the cause

An alternative to this is to provide the children with given effects and ask them to add the cause. For example:

- The boy was late for school because . . .
- The sun was blacked out because . . .
- Because . . . the water froze.

3 Cause and effect cloze

A cloze activity can be devised that requires the children to add either the causes and/or the effects to a passage. For example: Goldilocks walked into the bears' home because . . . She felt hungry so . . . When she sat in baby bear's chair . . . because . . .

4 Match up

Various causes and effects are written on separate pieces of card and jumbled up, see next page. The children must match the cause to the appropriate effect.

5 Reverse thinking

The children are given a series of related causes and effects and they must restate without altering the initial relationship either using because, so or therefore. For example:

- Goldilocks fell asleep on baby bear's bed because she was tired. *Restate using therefore:* Goldilocks was tired therefore she fell asleep on baby bear's bed.
- There was limited land suitable for farming so attempts were made to cross the mountains. *Restate using because.*
- The freezing point of water is 0 degrees celsius therefore ice forms in puddles on extremely cold days. *Restate using because.*

Figure 6.1: Match up cards

 e.g.

because they come from different types of bedrock.	Granite is hard to break
because quartz is harder than these.	Stones along a river bed are smooth
because the water wears them smooth.	Glass and steel can be scratched by quartz
because it is made from crystals.	Stones look and feel different

6 Join up

The children search either shared books, jointly constructed texts or teacher constructed texts to find the common vocabulary used to link causes and effects *or* to find the words used to join two or more ideas.

7 Please explain

In groups the children are given topics to explain either orally or in written form. For example:

- Why fish can't survive out of water.
- How rain clouds are formed.
- Why Goldilocks caused the three bears to be angry.
- Why we are not permitted to run in the corridor.

8 Tell us how or why

The children list events, occasions or things that they would like explained. For example:

- How does a telephone work?
- Why does cork float?

- Why is there a hole in the ozone layer?
- How do detergents affect our water system?

Individuals or groups select or are allocated one of these to research and explain to the remainder of the grade. This can also be run in the same manner as 'Ask the Expert' (see page 26 for details).

9 Role play

The children are given a situation and, in groups, each member assumes the role of one of the people in the situation and tries to explain why the incident occurred. For example: 'Two children are playing cricket in their back yard when the ball breaks their neighbour's window. Explain how this happened from the batsman's and bowler's point of view'.

Emphasise that the explanation each participant gives will be influenced by particular interests, opinions and viewpoints. This could lead on to a discussion on how fact and opinions can affect explanations.

Assessment and evaluation of explanation writing

This is a suggested summary of aspects you may wish to use for your own particular evaluation needs. They may help you to set specific objectives for this aspect of your language programme. The selection of objectives will be dependent on the language development of the children you teach. Does the student attempt to write explanations in his or her own writing? Is the student able to:

- identify a cause and effect relationship?
- plan for the writing of explanations?
- write an explanation using cause and effect?
- write the explanation in logical sequence?
- use diagrams, illustrations, labels, charts etc. when writing an explanation?
- include sufficient information to enable the explanation to be easily followed?

Exploring explanations—a sample unit

This sample unit includes ideas for modelling sessions to be used within a language lesson. The modelling time would take no more than fifteen to twenty minutes. The suggestions for further activities

Down, Roundabout and Up Again
The Life of a River

Jim Howes
Illustrated by Frank Knight

would take extra time and may or may not be added to the modelling session time. They may be conducted in separate sessions with individual children, groups or the whole class.

Demonstration book:

Down, Roundabout and Up Again by Jim Howes (Southern Cross Series, Macmillan, 1987).

Session One

> **Focus**—Introduction to the book and to the function of subtitles

- Show the children the cover of the book but ensure that the subtitle is covered both on the cover and on the title page.
- Ask the children to predict what the book is about after
  - ▷ looking at the cover
  - ▷ turning to the title page and reading the Table of Contents
  - ▷ flicking through the pages of the book.
- Uncover the subtitle to confirm or refute the children's predictions. Discuss the function of subtitles.
- Children predict what may be included in the book and write what they would like explained in a book about rivers. Refer to this as the book is read over the next few sessions.

Further activities

Collect and display books that include a title and a subtitle and allow the children to browse and read these. They may wish to share their opinions on why the titles and subtitles are so written.

- Set up a 'What We Know About Rivers' chart and add facts to this as the book is read.
- Provide a display of books and poems about rivers.

Session Two

> **Focus**—Locating the cause and effect in the text

- Share Chapter 1 with the children. Have the children explain the reasons for the following after reading the text. Frame each question so the children have to make connections between cause and effect. Ensure they use logical thought and expression.
  - ▷ Why are there no tall trees?
  - ▷ How do the soaks help the animals survive in the high country?
  - ▷ The plants are low growing because . . .

▷ . . . therefore the cattle don't overgraze the paddocks.

• Share Chapter 2 and ask the children to explain why this section of the river is like it is. Ensure they give a reason for each of the phenomena. They may need to refer back to the book to clarify their thoughts.

   Some of the reasons for the phenomena are not given so pose some questions that will require reflection and reasoning. For example:

▷ Why would the water be cold?

▷ How would the trees stop the soil from falling into the rivers?

▷ Why would the platypus not wish to be seen?

Further activities

• Search the text for those words that link cause and effect or that join two or more ideas.

• Continue adding to the 'What We Know About Rivers' chart.

Session Three

Focus — How an explanation is constructed

• Share with the children Chapter 4 'A World of its Own' and ask them what this chapter explained.

• Share Chapter 5 but at the end of selected paragraphs have the children suggest the main reason for the grouping of the information. This can be done individually or with partners. Share their opinions and discuss the reasons for their judgements.

• Emphasise the way the paragraphs have been printed. They are not indented so how can the reader tell that it is a paragraph?

Further activities

• Reread paragraphs from any section of the book that has already been presented to the children and jointly construct a written retelling of the paragraph.

• Have the children select one of the paragraphs from the book that they have already read and rewrite it in their own words. This can be a small group or partner activity.

• Read paragraphs to the children and have them provide headings for the content.

Session Four

Focus — Exploring the structure of explanations using oral retelling

Introduce the children to the oral-to-oral retelling procedure using the last chapter in the book, 'The End of the Trail'. This modified activity helps children gain an understanding of the structure of explanations and is based on the read and retell procedure.

Prior to the session mask the text in this chapter but allow the heading and illustrations to be seen. Ask the children to predict what will be explained in the chapter. Read the chapter to the children and allow them to check their predictions. The title of the chapter can now be unmasked.

Explain to the children that you are going to read the chapter again and that you would like them to listen carefully as you wish them to attempt a joint, continuous oral retelling at the end of your reading.

At the completion of the reading children can volunteer to retell the content in the correct sequence. As a child is retelling a section the others must be critical listeners.

Further activities

- Have the children select one of the chapters of the book that they have already read and retell the explanation in their own words. This can be a small group or partner activity.
- Discuss the use of the inverted commas in this text (for the words mouth, edge, clock and trail) and have the children give definitions for each of these words using the information in the text as the basis of the definition.

Session Five

Focus—Jointly constructing an explanation

Model the writing of an explanation about a familiar subject. Perhaps the schoolyard could be divided into different sections (adventure playground, oval, passive activity area, canteen area etc.) and each section then written about to explain its features and function. Stress the importance of not just writing a description but adding the reasons for the features etc.

Further activities

- Use the map at the front of *Down, Roundabout and Up Again* and mark in the places as mentioned in the book.
- Write an explanation of the water cycle as it is presented in the book.
- Compile a chart to list what the author needed to know to be able to write the book.
- In groups complete the explanation commenced in session five.

Books to further explore explanations with the children

BB   This indicates that a book is also available in big book format.

Aliki. *How A Book Is Made*. Bodley, 1986.

Aliki. *Fossils Tell of Long Ago*. Black, 1973.

Burgess, Jan. *The Heart & Blood*. Macmillan, 1988.

Clark, Phillip (ed.). *You & Your Body*. Macmillan, 1979.

Croser, Josephine. *The Life of a Duck*. Magic Bean In-Fact Series, Era Publications, 1989. **BB**

Drew, David. *Body Facts*. Nelson, 1989.

Drew, David. *Body Maps*. Nelson, 1989.

Drew, David. *Small Worlds*. Nelson, 1989.

Gibbons, Gail. *Up Goes the Skyscraper!* Four Winds Press, 1986.

Ingram, Ann Bower. *Making a Picture Book*. Methuen, 1987.

Kovacs Buxbaum, Susan & Golden Gelman, Rita. *Body Noises*. Hamish Hamilton, 1984.

Martin, Rodney. *The First Lunar Landing*. Era Publications, 1990. **BB**

Mayle, Peter. *Why Are We Getting A Divorce?* Harmony, n.d.

Oleksy, Walter. *Experiments With Heat*. Children's Press, 1986.

Parker, Steve. *The Ear and Hearing*. Franklin Watts, 1989.

Parker, Steve. *The Eye and Seeing*. Franklin Watts, 1989.

Pollock, John. *On Site*. Bookshelf, Martin Educational, 1987. **BB**

Skidmore, Steve. *Poison! Beware!* Collins Dove, 1990.

Smith, Katherine, A. *How Cows Make Milk*. Magic Bean In-Fact Series, Era Publications, 1989. **BB**

Smith, Katherine, A. *A Check Up with The Doctor*. Magic Bean In-Fact Series, Era Publications, 1989. **BB**

Suzuki, David. *Looking at Insects. Activities for Kids*. Allen and Unwin, 1989.

Thompson, Ruth. *Making a Book*. Franklin Watts, 1987.

Whitfield, Dr Philip & Pope, Joyce. *Why Do the Seasons Change?* Hamish Hamilton, 1987.

Yardley, Thomas. *Down The Plughole—Explore Your Plumbing*. Collins Dove, 1990.

PERSUASIVE WRITING

•••

Description

Persuasive writing involves stating beliefs in such a way as to try and convince others to accept a point of view. The information is presented in a form appropriate to the audience to be convinced and the writer needs to be well versed in the subject.

Persuasive writing may involve a 'one-eyed' or biased approach to an issue or may involve the stating and consideration of all points of view on an issue.

There are different types of persuasive writing which are used for different purposes and audiences. For example, persuasive writing can be used for the purposes listed on the next page.

Provide opportunities for children to use persuasive writing in the form of arguments or debates.

- To promote and sell goods, services, activities etc. (for example, advertisements).
- To change people's points of view or attitudes by putting forward an argument about a specific issue (for example, 'All schools should have recycling facilities for community use.').
- To plead a case (for example, 'Save the Rainforests').

One form of persuasive writing is the argument. This form requires the stating of an issue, the stand being taken by the author, the reasons for the particular stance plus a recommended solution. For example:

Each year hundreds of Australians are slaughtered on our roads. *← statement of issue of concern*

Many of these are victims of drunk drivers or were indeed drunk drivers themselves. In my opinion the laws need to be changed to make it illegal to drink and drive. *← statement of opinion*

The Law at present allows a driver to drink as long as they don't exceed a given alcohol blood level. Unfortunately the drink-drivers are often unable to judge the level of alcohol in their blood so they continue to drive. *← Arguments to support opinion*

Some drivers appear to be influenced by alcohol more quickly than others so perhaps the present legal blood alcohol limit could be too high for some people.

I would like to see a review of the current law and appropriate *← Recommendation for a solution* changes made to ban all drink-driving.

Debates, which are conducted orally, are a form of argument in which two opposing points of view are stated and both sides are argued. Supporting evidence for each side is put forward and finally an informed opinion is stated based on the two arguments.

The written form of a debate can be modelled in which the issue is stated, the arguments for and against the issue are listed and finally a statement on the author's stand on the issue is made after both arguments are considered. For example:

The local community is divided over the proposal to build in the *← statement of the issue* town area a fast-food store belonging to one of the world's largest fast-food chains. Should the proposal be denied?

Firstly, the fast-food chain will bring opportunities for part-time employment for many of the young people in the area. *← Argument to support the proposal* Employment opportunities in this local area are very limited.

Secondly, the establishment of the store will provide a service which is lacking in this area. There are only limited choices of fast-food outlets in the local community (one fish and chip shop and one pizza shop).

Argument against the proposal

The opposing view is that the fast-food outlet will alter the quiet atmosphere of the area because it will encourage people out of the area to come and buy at the store.

Another point to be considered is the 'visual pollution' it will create with its large neon signs and huge advertising hoardings. Because this area is concerned with all conservation issues this could be the beginning of the wrecking of the local environment.

Conclusion after the consideration of both points of view

After considering both sides of the argument, it is my opinion that the proposal to build a fast-food store should be supported. A fast-food store would be an asset to the local area as it will provide employment for the local residents as well as encouraging people outside the area to come and use the store and perhaps generate more spending in the other stores. The visual pollution is not a relevant issue because all the other shops in the area have advertising signs of some description and the local council can enforce restrictions on the size and type of hoarding used.

Another form of persuasive writing is the advertisement, which can use many different strategies to persuade the reader that they are making the right choice. For example:

Posing question in reader's mind

Do you have rough, calloused feet?

personalised

Well here's the answer for you!

repetition of the product name

PEDISMOOTH. The beauty treatment for your feet! Millions of feet can't be wrong!

The 30 cm long handle means no more bending and the waterproof coating means PEDISMOOTH can be used in the bath or shower.

simplification of process

Just rub the PEDISMOOTH applicator over your feet and the rough skin and callouses will disappear.

Use of famous person to promote product

Tina Toeby uses PEDISMOOTH daily for smooth pretty feet.

Buy PEDISMOOTH now before stocks run out.

Don't your feet deserve PEDISMOOTH?

Feeling of urgency

Available at all good chemists.

PEDISMOOTH. The beauty treatment for your feet.

Learning experiences for persuasive writing

- Take advantage of relevant authentic opportunities as they arise to introduce persuasive writing to the children because it is a form that few children would have in their writing repertoire or would attempt on their own.
- Use actual experiences as the basis of the modelling process to ensure that the children see a real purpose for this form of writing. For example:
  ▷ To plead a case (letters to the principal or school council with regard to school issues).
  ▷ To promote goods or services (advertisement writing to promote the school fete, cake stalls, a school concert etc.).
  ▷ To put forward an argument (school uniforms should be compulsory).
- Use opportunities in other curriculum areas to model persuasive writing. For example:
  ▷ Health—brochures about the dangers of smoking etc.
  ▷ Environmental Studies—letters to the relevant authorities to remedy local problems.
  ▷ Social Education—writing debates about issues.
- Use children's literature to develop the children's understanding of persuasive writing techniques. For example:
  ▷ John Burmingham's *Oi! Get Off Our Train* is a delightful picture story-book that mentions animals whose survival is threatened by human activity. This may be a way of providing a basis for writing persuasive texts about animal conservation and care of the environment.
  ▷ Shel Silverstein's *The Giving Tree* could provide the stimulus to discuss the importance and need for trees. This could lead to writing letters to local authorities to encourage them to provide tree planting programmes or for the children to write arguments for and against logging programmes. It may even stimulate the collection of the information from conservation organisations and logging companies and the subsequent analysis of their separate arguments.
- List the techniques that are used in persuasive writing to convince the reader that the argument given is the best option. For example:
  ▷ appealing to the emotions of the reader
  ▷ using thought-provoking questions
  ▷ repetition of words, phrases, concepts etc.
  ▷ analysing opposing points of view.
- Talk about the techniques that are unacceptable and should not be used in persuasive writing. For example:

> ▷ distortion of the truth to suit the writer's point of view
> ▷ deliberate omission of important information so readers can't make an informed judgement
> ▷ undesirable human characteristics promoted as desirable (greed, violence, cruelty etc.).

- Discuss the various devices used in some advertisements. For example:
  > ▷ excessive use of adjectives
  > ▷ repetition of words, phrases etc.
  > ▷ slogans and catchy sayings
  > ▷ catchy rhythm or patterns in writing
  > ▷ exaggeration
  > ▷ the use of questions
  > ▷ appealing to the emotions of the reader through his or her ego
  > ▷ the use of stereotypes
  > ▷ the quoting of authorities or famous people
  > ▷ the simplification of the process or product being promoted
  > ▷ the call for action, the expression of urgency to act on the advice offered in the advertisement
  > ▷ the posing of a perceived problem and the suggestion of a solution.

- Guide the children's understanding of the purpose and structure of advertisements by asking questions such as these when advertisements are being discussed:
  > ▷ What is the message of the advertisement?
  > ▷ How is the message presented?
  > ▷ What devices are used to convey the message?

- Collect a series of advertisements and discuss the use of the print, graphics, set out, size etc. to convey the message.

- Look at the language used in advertisements and list all the 'persuasive words' and the devices used to sway the reader's judgement.

Focus the children's attention on the various persuasive strategies used in written advertisements.

- Provide plenty of opportunities for the children to share opinions and ideas before and during the writing process involved in persuasive writing.
- Mention that some persuasive writing may appeal only to the emotions and not present any factual information.
- Emphasise the need to organise reasons for a particular point of view when planning to write a persuasive text in the form of an argument.
- Discuss the need to take a stand on an issue or make a judgement before attempting to write a persuasive text.
- Model the different formats of a written argument. For example:
  ▷ Stress the need to state the issue and stand being argued, the reasons for a particular stance and a recommended solution.
  ▷ Model an argument in which an issue and both sides of the issue are examined and the stand of the author is then written.
- Conduct oral debates in which the children must prepare arguments that are supported by evidence (examples, statistics etc.). Emphasise the importance of anticipating the arguments of the opposition and create responses for these.

Activities for persuasive writing

1 Point of view activities

- Write responses, stating one's own point of view, to issues at school, home or in the community. For example:
  ▷ Swap cards at school.
  ▷ The use of animals to test cosmetics etc.
- Provide groups of three children with a description of a situation or incident. Each child assumes the role of one of the participants in the situation and gives his or her point of view or account of the event. For example:
  ▷ The pros and cons of keeping a stray dog that followed a child home from school as stated by the child, the mother and the dog.

2 Cartoon comments

- Collect cartoons that make comments about issues. Discuss the meaning conveyed through the illustration and the limited text. Does this reveal the opinion of the cartoonist?
- Encourage the children to create cartoons that will reflect a situation at school and perhaps will reveal their feelings about it. For example: the removal of trees to create more playground; or the school bully and his activities.

3 Search and compare activities

Conduct a search for the different types of persuasive writing on the same subject. For example:

- Smoking—collect information from the tobacco companies, the Anti-cancer Council, etc. and compare the writing.

4 Audience writing

Write a piece of persuasive writing about the same issue but targeted to different audiences. For example, the wearing of helmets by bike riders. Write a text to be read by the young bike rider, the parents, the law makers or the manufacturers.

5 Advertisement activities

- Study a selection of advertisements and rate on a continuum labelled 'Information' at one end and 'Persuasion' at the other.
- The children write an advertisement for their homes using the format in the real estate section of the paper.
- The children write their own television, radio or printed advertisement for objects.
- Read the property section in the daily paper and try to write what the ad *really* means (reading between the lines). For example 'a renovator's delight' could mean a very run-down building.

6 Crazy products

Present the children with a creative problem-solving activity and have them work in groups to develop imaginative solutions for the problem. For example:

- Pose the problem that a toothpaste manufacturer is concerned that sales are down and needs a product and an effective advertising campaign to boost sales. The children, in groups, devise a plan of action, agree on a suitable product, design the packaging and then write a newspaper advertisement for the product.
- Extend the children's creative problem-solving ability by asking them to create a product for an imaginary purpose. For example, a trap for dinosaurs. The children write an advertisement to promote the product.

7 I'm great!

The children write a promotional text about themselves and mention all (and only) their strong features.

Assessment and evaluation of persuasive writing

This is a suggested summary of aspects you may wish to use for your own particular evaluation needs. They may help you to set specific objectives for this aspect of your language programme. The selection of objectives will be dependent on the language development of the children you teach. The student is able to:

- identify different forms of persuasive writing:
  - ▷ advertising
  - ▷ arguments
  - ▷ opinions or stating a point of view.
- identify and concisely state a problem.
- write own opinion on issues.
- select and write facts to support a point of view.
- arrange facts in logical sequence writing the strongest support first.
- use variety of strategies to persuade the audience.
- identify the difference between fact and opinion.
- write advertisements using the appropriate strategies and devices.
- identify unacceptable techniques in persuasive writing.

Exploring persuasive writing— a sample unit

This sample unit includes ideas for modelling sessions to be used within a language lesson. The modelling time would take no more than fifteen to twenty minutes. The suggestions for further activities would take extra time and may or may not be added to the modelling session time. They may be conducted in separate sessions with individual children, groups or the whole class.

Note that this Unit of Work uses two different types of books to help develop the children's understanding of the different forms and purposes of persuasive writing.

Demonstration books:

A Pet For Mrs Arbuckle by Gwenda Smyth and Ann James (Puffin Books, 1989)
This book is not in big book format so multiple copies may need to be used to enable the children to view the selected examples of text.

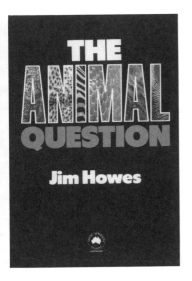

The Animal Question by Jim Howes (Nelson, 1985)
This book is not in big book format. It is not essential the children see the text because the actual modelling of persuasive writing comes from the activities arising from the text.

Session One

> **Focus**—Introduction to *A Pet For Mrs Arbuckle* and to the concept of persuasion

- From the cover the children may predict the type and content of book.
- Read the book to the children.
- Discuss the following questions:
  - ▷ Why did the gingernut cat want to travel with Mrs Arbuckle?
  - ▷ What did each animal do when Mrs Arbuckle arrived to interview them? Why?
  - ▷ What did the cat do each time Mrs Arbuckle was interested in a particular animal as a pet? Why?
  - ▷ When the gingernut cat added a comment about each animal what did Mrs Arbuckle do? Why?
- The discussion arising from the responses to these questions should enable the teacher to introduce the concept of 'persuasion' and to locate and discuss examples in the story.

Further activities

- Collect pictures of other animals, not mentioned in the book, and ask the children to write reasons why each would or would not be a good pet.
- In groups of three the children assume the following roles:
  - ▷ An animal that wishes to be Mrs Arbuckle's pet (one not already mentioned in the book).
  - ▷ Mrs Arbuckle, who would like the particular animal as a pet.
  - ▷ The gingernut cat who would not like the animal to be Mrs Arbuckle's pet.

  Each character must put forward an argument for their point of view.

Session Two

> **Focus**—The structure and purpose of advertisements

- Refer to the wanted advertisement Mrs Arbuckle placed in the newspaper in an effort to find a suitable pet. Ask the following questions:

▷ Under which section of the newspaper would it be placed?

▷ Why was it so brief?

▷ What is missing from the advertisement that would need to be included in real advertisements?

• Look at the classified advertisements section in a newspaper and discuss the following:

▷ the various classifications used

▷ the purpose of the different types of classified advertisements.

• Discuss the structure of each type of advertisement and focus on the following:

▷ Why the use of abbreviations?

▷ The choice of words. How are they selected?

▷ The use of print. What size print? What type of print? Why?

▷ The use of graphics.

Further activities

• Model the writing of a wanted advertisement to be placed in the newspaper.

Session Three

> **Focus**—The characteristics and structure of an argument and writing to present one point of view (using the demonstration book *The Animal Question*).

• Read the section on 'Factory Farming' (pages 37 to last paragraph on page 39).

• List and discuss the following:

▷ the reasons given for factory farming

▷ the reasons given against factory farming.

• Use some of the arguments given for and against factory farming and model an argument against it, ensuring the following structure of an argument is modelled:

▷ The issue and the writer's stand are stated clearly.

▷ Points against factory farming are written in order of importance and evidence or reasons for these are stated.

▷ The stand of the writer is stated again at the conclusion of the argument.

Further activities

• Using the reasons given for factory farming write an argument supporting it using the above model as a guide.

• Read the letters on pages 35 and 36 about animal experimentation and, using the reasons given in each letter, write arguments for or against this procedure.

- In groups the children can read the Letters to the Editor section of the newspaper and collect those that put forward a point of view.

Session Four

> **Focus**—Writing to discuss all sides of an argument, its structure and function

- Use the points of view on factory farming stated by each party; model a discussion that puts both sides and then gives the stand of the writer. Ensure that:
  - ▷ the issue is stated clearly
  - ▷ arguments for and against the issue are stated
  - ▷ the conclusion reveals the opinion of the writer.

Further activities

- In groups the children prepare a written discussion on an issue of school concern. For example:
  - ▷ the wearing of school uniforms
  - ▷ the sale of junk food at the canteen
  - ▷ whether or not school camps are necessary.
- Use opportunities as they arise in school curriculum to write discussions. For example:
  - ▷ Health—Should sunscreens be tax free?
  - ▷ Environmental Education—Grafitti on public buildings is very common. Should it be regarded as a work of art or should the 'artists' be made to clean it off?
  - ▷ Literature—Was Goldilocks just an inquisitive little girl or was she a deliberate little vandal?

Session Five

> **Focus**—Argument to plead a case. The writing of a text to state an issue of concern and a suggested course of action.

- Use the information revealed in 'Factory Farming' to model the writing of a letter to appropriate authorities to recommend a stop to battery farming. Ensure that the letter includes the following:
  - ▷ the issue causing concern
  - ▷ the reasons for the concern
  - ▷ recommendation for action to stop battery farming.

Further activities

- Use current issues and write a piece of persuasive writing about one in any form of argument (to put forward a point of view, to present both sides of an argument and to plead a case). For example the children may write on any of the following:
  ▷ clearing rainforests
  ▷ duck shooting season
  ▷ the use of fossil fuels
  ▷ driftnet fishing.
  ▷ animal experimentation for cosmetics
  ▷ the use of animals for scientific and medical experiments
  ▷ the use of animal fur for coats etc.
- Use issues related to school and have the children write in any of the forms of persuasive writing to present a point of view.

• •

Books to further explore persuasive writing with the children

BB   This indicates that a book is also available in big book format.

Please note that there appears to be very few children's books that use this form of writing. It may be necessary to use other sources (magazines, newspapers, letters to the editor, advertising material, pamphlets, brochures, cartoons, bumper stickers, jingles, slogans, graffiti etc. or persuasive writing from organisations).

Some children's literature includes small passages of persuasive writing according to the plot of the story while other children's literature will provide a range of creative and imaginative persuasive writing activities through which the characteristics and analysis of this writing form can be modelled by the teacher and explored by the children. For example:

Baker, Jeannie. *Where the Forest Meets the Sea*. Julia MacRae, 1987.
Barton, Miles. *Animal Rights*. Watts, 1987.
Burmingham, John. *Oi! Get Off Our Train*. Jonathan Cape, 1989.
Cleary, Beverley. *Dear Mr Henshaw*. Puffin, 1983.
Gray, Nigel. *I'll Take You to Mrs Cole*. Macmillan, 1985.
McLeod, Doug (Ed.). *The Southern Cross Herald*. Macmillan, 1987. **BB**
Silverstein, Shel. *The Giving Tree*. Jonathan Cape, 1986.
Smyth, Gwenda, & James, Ann. *A Hobby For Mrs Arbuckle*. Viking Kestrel, Penguin, 1989.
Stewart, Maureen. *Dear Emily*. Puffin, 1987.

◆8◆
NARRATIVE INFORMATION
▼

Description

Narrative information refers to those texts that use a narrative structure to convey factual information. The factual information may be woven around a particular event, character, thing or setting. For example:

At the end of five weeks one egg was bad but inside the other a baby female Fairy Penguin struggled to be free. She scraped against the shell, using the egg tooth on the end of her bill backwards and forwards, backwards and forwards, until the shell broke open. She was warm beneath the penguin belly, her downy coat of feathers too thin yet to keep out the cold.*

Narrative information is included in the factual section of this book because the authors of such texts use the narrative structure to impart facts. The planning for writing narrative information texts requires the same planning, researching and preparation as for any other factual writing. Narrative information books may be regarded as fictional efforts but, for the purposes of exploring the structure of these texts, I have put them in the category of factual texts.

Fictionalised biography is included in this category because facts are used as the basis of the narrative but the action and dialogue is the product of the writer's imagination. One such example is *Louis Braille—The Boy Who Invented Books for the Blind* by Margaret Davidson.

* From *The Penguin that Walks at Night* by Pauline Reilly, pp. 14–15

Learning experiences for narrative information

- Discuss the differences between narrative information and other narrative texts. For example:
  ▷ Narrative information involves the inclusion of facts that are woven into a well structured narrative.
  ▷ The factual information is conveyed to the reader through the use of the characters, events, situations, setting or objects included in the story.
  ▷ The settings or descriptions used can be real or written in such a way that they are believable.
  ▷ Some narrative information texts include information that is general and all-encompassing (for example *Longneck's Billabong* by Ann Coleridge).
  ▷ Some narrative information texts include specific information about an event, person, living thing, issue etc. (for example *The Castle Hill Uprising* by Margaret Pearce).
- Read as many examples of narrative information to the children as possible.
- Set up a display of narrative information books that are written about the following:
  ▷ animals
  ▷ events
  ▷ people.
- Select one example of a narrative information text and collect other examples of writing about the factual part of the narrative information. For example:
  Select the narrative information book The Message Of The Dance *by Anne Coleridge. Find all forms of narrative and factual texts about bees. (The basis of the factual information in the above narrative information text.) Discuss and compare the different writing forms.*
- When planning to write a narrative information text model the use of the research strategies used for factual text writing (see pages 30, 31 and 32 for details).
- Link narrative information to the content areas of the curriculum. For example:
  ▷ As part of Social Studies: write the diary of a sailor on an old sailing vessel.
  ▷ As part of Health Studies: weave a story around the work of Louis Pasteur, Florence Nightingale, Louis Braille etc.

▷ As part of Environmental Studies: use the information you have found out about water pollution and create a story that will include this.

• Set the children the task of writing about a particular type of narrative information text. For example:

▷ Write about an event (for example a narrative information text about the landing on the moon).

▷ Write about a person (for example, imagine you are the inventor of the telephone, the first car, a flying machine etc.).

▷ Write about an issue (for example conservation — write about recycling goods).

▷ Write about an animal (for example, about an endangered animal).

Assessment and evaluation of narrative information writing

This is a suggested summary of aspects you may wish to use for your own particular evaluation needs. They may help you to set specific objectives for this aspect of your language programme. The selection of objectives will be dependent on the language development of the children you teach. The student is able to:

• recognise narrative information.
• distinguish the facts from the fiction in narrative information.
• plan for narrative information writing.
• research for information.
• weave factual information around a character, setting or an event.

Exploring narrative information — a sample unit

This sample unit includes ideas for modelling sessions to be used within a language lesson. The modelling time would take no more than fifteen to twenty minutes. The suggestions for further activities would take extra time and may or may not be added to the modelling session time. They may be conducted in separate sessions with individual children, groups or the whole class.

Demonstration book:

Longneck's Billabong by Ann Coleridge (Southern Cross Series, Macmillan, 1987). Also available in big book format.

Session One

> **Focus**—Introduction to the book and to the characteristics of narrative information texts

- Show the children the cover of the book and ask them to predict the content.
- Read the book in its entirety to the children. Allow time for them to discuss the illustrations and the content.
- Ask the children to describe how the book was written and what type of book it is. Introduce them to the term 'narrative information' and its features.

Further activities

- Set up a display of factual and narrative books about tortoises.
- Make a chart which lists all the creatures that lived in the billabong.
- Refer to the book to draw food chains related to the creatures mentioned in the book.
- Collect examples of other narrative information texts and share these with the children.
- Study the use of descriptions in the book.
- Talk about the way the information was grouped.
- Make a model of a billabong and add the creatures.

Session Two

> **Focus**—How the author may have planned for the writing of the book

- Ask the children what they learnt about tortoises after reading the book and record this information. Refer to the book as required.
- Focus on the author's planning for the book by asking these questions:
  - ▷ How did the author give us this information?
  - ▷ What did the author need to know before he could write the book?
- How would he have planned for the writing of this book?

Planning before writing is an important part of the writing pocess.

Further activities

- Draw a time line to represent the events in Longneck's life and include the facts for each event.
- Compile a chart 'What We Know About Tortoises'. This is added to as the children read the books on display.
- Select any passage in the book and write the facts that the author included in it.

Session Three

> **Focus**—Planning for a jointly constructed narrative information text

- Plan to write a narrative information text about a creature mentioned in *Longneck's Billabong* (for example frogs).
- List the factual information the children would like to include in the story.
- List the information the children already know about the creature.
- Compile questions to guide the children in their research.
- List the sources of information the children could use.
- List the research tasks that will need to be completed before the writing can commence.

Further activities

- Set up a Fact Tree to record all the facts the children research about frogs.

Session Four

> **Focus**—Collecting and organising information for writing

- Model reading for information using the guiding questions.
- Read a factual text about the creature the text is going to be about and build a Fact Tree.
- Group the information under headings (Food, Habitat, Enemies, Description etc.).
- Talk about the way this factual information could be included in a narrative information text.

Further activities

- Keep adding new found information to the charts.
- Reread *Longneck's Billabong* and focus on the structure of the text. Ask the following questions:
  - ▷ What facts are included in the beginning, middle and ending of the story?
  - ▷ Is there any event in the story that could not happen?
  - ▷ Is there any information that is not fact?
  - ▷ How did the author tell you about the tortoise's food, enemies, lifecycle, habitat etc?
  - ▷ How did the author indicate the passing of time in the story?

Session Five

> **Focus**—Drafting a narrative information text

- Draw a story map to show the sequence of events to be included in the text. Try to match the facts that have been researched to the appropriate event.
- Jointly construct the first draft of the text.
- Think aloud as you write. Demonstrate how writers plan for, write, reread, rework and alter their drafts.

Further activities

- The children may complete the above draft individually or in groups or further focus sessions could be used to jointly construct the text.
- A big book could be published using the above text.
- The children can divide into groups and using the modelled procedure plan, research and write a narrative information text about another animal.

◆ The children can attempt a narrative information text based on the facts from one of the other content areas.

Books to further explore narrative information with the children

BB   This indicates that a book is also available in big book format.

Boddy, Michael. *The Smallest Frog In the World*. Lansdowne Press, 1980.

Catterwell, Thelma. *Sebastian Lives in a Hat*. Omnibus, 1989.

Chapman, Jean. *The Wreck of the Georgette*. Southern Cross Series, Macmillan, 1987.

Coleridge, Ann. *The Message of the Dance*. Southern Cross Series, Macmillan, 1989. **BB**

Cowcher, Helen. *Antarctica*. Georgian House, 1990.

Gibson, Helen. *Woorayl the Lyrebird*. Southern Cross Series, Macmillan, 1987.

Giono, Jean. *The Man who Planted Trees*. Collins, 1989.

Glimmerveen, Ulco. *A Tale Of Antarctica*. Ashton Scholastic, 1990.

Hautzig, Esther. *The Endless Steppe*. Penguin, 1969.

Kerr, Judith. *When Hitler Stole Pink Rabbit*. Lions, 1974.

Morris, Jill. *Numbat Run*. Harcourt Brace Jovanovich, 1989. **BB**

Pearce, Margaret. *The Castle Hill Uprising*. Southern Cross Series, Macmillan, 1987.

Pigdon, Nancye. *Magnet Magic*. Southern Cross Series, Macmillan, 1989.

Rees, Leslie. *The Story of Two Thumbs the Koala*. Child & Associates, 1988.

Rees, Leslie. *The Story of Kurri Kurri the Kookaburra*. Child & Associates, 1988.

Reece, James. *Lester and Clyde*. Ashton Scholastic, 1990. **BB**

Reilly, Pauline. *The Penguin that Walks at Night*. Kangaroo Press, 1985.

Wheatley, Nadia. *My Place*. Collins Dove, 1987.

RECOUNTS

▼

Description

A recount consists of the reconstruction of a past experience or event; usually one in which the author has been involved, although there are some recounts that are imaginative and are not written within the author's experiences. The information in all recounts is arranged in a time sequence with appropriate language usage to link the events and to show the passing of time. A recount may involve the stating of observations and the inclusion of a personal comment. Usually a recount quickly establishes, within the introduction: the time, setting and participants in the event to be described. Recounts can be about real or imaginary events.

when ⟍
who ⟍

Last week the grade six children spent three days on a school ⟵————— *brisk introduction*

camp at Wilsons Promontory which is a National Park on the

why southern-most tip of Victoria. ⟵————————————— *where*

We travelled to the camp by bus and on arrival at the camp

site set up our tents and then spent the rest of the day exploring

the surrounding area.

On the second day we participated in a long hike up to the ⟵————— *events in sequence*

summit of the tallest mountain on the Promontory. It was a very

hot and tiring walk but the view from the summit was the reward

for persevering.

Events in sequence →

(On the morning) of the last day of the camp we rose early and packed, ready for the long journey home.

(During) the trip home several of the children fell asleep. On arrival back at school (we) raced off the bus to be greeted by (our)

Comment or judgement →

parents. On the whole the camp was a great success.

use of pronouns

Recount writing is one of the most common forms of writing used by children. It is the teacher's responsibility to expose children to a range of well structured and interesting models so that they improve the quality and structure of their own recounts.

Learning experiences for recounts

- Discuss the point that recounts usually require a swift introduction to the participants, setting and time of the event to be recounted.
- Provide practice for the children to recall, in correct sequence, all the events of an intended recount.
- Model the writing of recounts and point out:
  ▷ the use of past tense
  ▷ the elimination of irrelevant details so that only the important aspects of the event are included.
  ▷ The use of personal pronouns in recounts in which the author was a participant.
  ▷ Some recounts can be of an imaginative origin.
- Emphasise the importance of breaking the event to be recounted into small, easily followed sequential steps.
- Provide practice for the children to recount personal experiences.
- Use school experiences as the source of models for recount writing. For example:
  ▷ Recall the sequence of events of a school excursion.
  ▷ At the end of a school day have the children write a recount of the day's events.
  ▷ During Morning Talk or Show and Tell sessions write up one of the children's news items as a recount.
  ▷ Use news items from the radio, TV or newspaper and write these as recounts.
  ▷ Observe and write a recount on a day in the life of the principal, librarian, a fellow classmate etc.
  ▷ Write a recount of a science procedure, maths activity, class activity etc.
- Discourage the excessive use of 'then' in children's recounts. Discuss the use of more interesting ways of ordering the events in the recount.

- Build up a collection of words that can be used instead of 'then' to denote the passing of time. List these on charts where children can refer to them as they are writing their own recounts (meanwhile, during, later, simultaneously, eventually, gradually, after, before etc.).
- Read examples of recounts and use these as opportunities to talk about the formation of the past tense of verbs. Locate and list all the verbs in a recount. Group these according to the way they are formed.
- Provide activities that will help develop the children's observation skills so they can record accurate recounts of events. For example:
  ▷ Set up short-term observation activities and ask children to record findings. For example, record what happened in the corridor over a five minute period.
  ▷ Plan long term activities to be recorded. For example, over a period of a week what were the changes to the house under construction across the road? Over a season what changes did you see in a given area of the garden?

Activities for recount writing

1 Recount board

A large sheet of paper is pinned up in the room on which the children are encouraged to write personal recounts. These can be read by the other class members to see if they make sense and that all the important details have been included.

2 Listen and recount

The children listen to a partner's telling of a personal experience and then orally recount this to a larger audience.

3 News recounts

In groups the children collect and read an interesting news item, write it as a recount and present it to the class.

4 Character recounts

The children select a character from a story they've read and proceed to write the events in the story in recount form from the character's point of view.

5 Point of view recounts

The children write an actual experience as a recount from the point of view of one of the participants. For example: write a recount of a school excursion as experienced by the teacher, a student, the bus driver, a parent etc.

6 Change the form

- Change a procedural text (for example, a recipe) into a recount of the process involved.
- Change the recount of an excursion into a realistic narrative.
- Change a narrative into a recount using the third person.

7 Change the person

The children are encouraged to write recounts in either the first or third person through the following activities:
- write or rewrite a recount in the third person
- write or rewrite a recount in the first person
- write an imaginative recount in first/third person.

8 Recount mural

Depicting events in sequence pictorially before writing often helps children order their thoughts so that a more detailed and interesting recount is created. For example:
- As a literature study activity the children, after reading a book, create a mural of the main events in the story. When this artistic interpretation is completed they add a written recount for each of the events depicted.
- Following a class excursion or special activity the children depict the event as a mural and then add the recount written in either the first or third person.

9 Stop and recount

This activity is designed to help develop the children's observation skills and their ability to recount accurately. For example:
- As an impromptu activity have the children stop their current activity and then recount what they were doing in the last session/lunch hour/five minutes etc.
- Conduct an activity in front of the children (or ask a fellow teacher or class members to do so) and without prior warning ask the children to recount what they observed.

Assessment and evaluation of recount writing

This is a suggested summary of aspects you may wish to use for your own particular evaluation needs. They may help you to set specific objectives for this aspect of your language programme. The selection of objectives will be dependent on the language development of the children you teach. The student is able to:

- write personal recounts.
- write imaginative recounts.
- write factual recounts.
- write events in sequence.
- quickly establish the participants, setting and time in a written recount.
- break the sequence of events in a recount into small interesting steps.
- identify and use personal pronouns in recounts of personal experiences.
- use a variety of words and phrases to designate time and the time links between events in the recount.
- identify recounts written in either the first or third person.

Exploring recounts—a sample unit

This sample unit includes ideas for modelling sessions to be used within a language lesson. The modelling time would take no more than fifteen to twenty minutes. The suggestions for further activities would take extra time and may or may not be added to the modelling session time. They may be conducted in separate sessions with individual children, groups or the whole class.

Demonstration book:

Coming Home—A Dog's True Story by Ted Harriot (Lynx, 1988).

Session One

> **Focus**—To introduce the book and the features of a recount

- Read the book to the children. Allow time for the children to

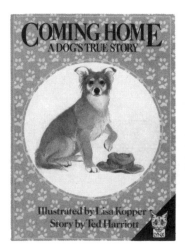

study the illustrations and to discuss the story at the end of the
reading.

- Guide the children to focus on the writing form used by asking
  the following questions:
  ▷ What was the purpose of the story?
  ▷ Who was telling the story?
  ▷ What events happened in the story?
  ▷ When did the story take place? How do you know?
  ▷ How do you think the author gained the information for the
    story?
- Introduce the term 'recount' and explain what the word means.
- Explain why this story can be referred to as a recount.

Further activities

- List words that begin with the prefix 're', which means back or
  again. Build up a chart of these words.
- Search newspapers for recounts.
- Set up a recount board where children can add their personal
  recounts.
- Find examples of recounts and share these with the children.

Session Two

> **Focus**—The language features in recounts

- Reread the beginning of the story to the children and ask them
  to tell you what information they gained from these first three
  pages. Stress the importance of quickly establishing the basis of
  the recounts.
- Ask the children to suggest, in sequence, the main events in the
  story.
- Scan the text and list the following:
  ▷ All the ways used in the story to link one event with another.
  ▷ All the words and phrases etc. used to denote the passing of
    time.
  ▷ All the personal pronouns in a section of the text. Compile a
    chart of these and add others as they are located in further
    reading and writing.

Further activities

- Build up a class chart of words that can designate the passing of
  time.
- Build up a class list of pronouns.

Session Three

> **Focus**—The use of the first and third person in recounts

- Discuss how this story was written as a personal recount and introduce the term 'first person'.
- Refer to the recounts the children may have shared and select those recounted in the first person.
- Introduce the term 'third person'.
- Retell the story as a recount in the third person.

Group writing provides a supportive learning environment as the children experiment with different writing forms.

Further activities

- Divide the children into groups and each group selects one of the people mentioned in the story and writes a recount of an event in the story from their point of view.
- Write a recount of the events in the story from the point of view of the lady who took Bodger home.
- Write a recount of Bodger's next week with his new owners.

Session Four

> **Focus**—Diary writing in recount form

- Discuss and list how we can permanently recall the important events in our lives.
- Introduce the use of diaries and journals.
- Discuss the happenings of the previous day or of a recent important event at school (excursion, guest, activity etc.).

- List the previous day's happenings and suggest suitable words to link the events.
- Write the beginning paragraph that will most efficiently and briskly establish the time, participants, setting and reason for the event to be recounted.

Further activities

- Collect and read other diaries and journals (both personal and published) and discuss the forms used apart from recounts.
- Select a story that has been read to the children and have them write part of the story in the form of a diary entry by one of the characters in the book.

Session Five

> **Focus**—The planning for and the writing of recounts

- The children select an event that has personal importance to them and list the important parts of the event in the sequence. They compose a good introductory paragraph and then write the event in an interesting recount form.

Extension activity

- After a shared experience, for example an excursion, a guest speaker, a special event in the classroom, have the children write the important events in sequence and then link them with well chosen words or phrases that designate time sequences.

Books to further explore recounts with the children

It is difficult to find children's books with suitable examples of simple recounts. It seems most authors prefer to elaborate on the basic recount structure or employ more detailed writing forms. It is a form of writing that most children use and we need to extend their repertoire of writing forms. Simple examples of recounts can be found in newspapers and magazines. Diaries, both published and unpublished, could provide good examples of recounts.

Fusillo, Archimede. *Memories of Sunday Cricket in the Street*. Southern Cross Series, Macmillan, 1987.

King, John Anthony. *An Uncommonly Fine Day*. Collins, 1988.

Voirst, Judith. *Alexander and the Terrible, Horrible, No Good, Very Bad Day*. Blue Gum, Angus and Robertson, 1986.

FICTION WRITING

The term fiction is used to refer to those texts that are written primarily to entertain, are the product of a creative imagination and do not need to be factual, although some fiction is based on aspects of fact. I have divided fiction into the following categories:

traditional fiction, which includes folk-tales, fairy-tales, myths and legends and fables;

modern fiction, which includes modern fantasy, and contemporary realistic fiction.

Fiction Writing can be presented in either poetry or prose forms. A study of poetry writing is not included in this book because this very creative form of writing requires an extensive exploration beyond the scope of this book, which primarily explores the many ways of writing prose.

The narrative form of traditional and modern fiction can be presented in picture story-books, simple short stories and longer stories with complicated plots.

Most narratives contain the following elements (although some short stories and picture story-books need not include all of these).

Orientation (introduction) in which the characters, setting and time of the story are established. Usually the answers to who?, when? and where? are provided in this part of a narrative.

Complication (middle) in which the situations, activities and events involving the main character are expanded upon. These events are written in a fluent and cohesive sequence.

Resolution (ending) in which the complication is resolved satisfactorily but not necessarily happily.

Most narratives are written either in the first or third person and incorporate the above elements.

Although the main purpose of fiction is to entertain and amuse the reader, it can also inform, instruct or explain at the same time. For example:

- Fables provide messages or instructions about certain behaviours as in *The Hare and the Tortoise*.
- Historical fiction usually uses authentic details of the era to add to the plausibility of the plot as in *Longtime Passing* by Hesba Brinsmead.

Learning experiences for narratives

- Read as many forms of narrative as possible to the children and discuss the structure of these when appropriate but never to the detriment of the children's enjoyment of the story.
- Focus on the plot, characterisation, setting and structure when reading and writing narratives but be aware that the children's first attempts at narrative writing will usually only include action and very little attention to setting or characterisation.
- Help the children plan for their writing of narratives by posing questions that will focus on plot, characterisation, setting or structure. For example:

Plot

- ▷ What is going to happen?
- ▷ What will happen first/next/last etc?
- ▷ Why will that happen?
- ▷ What words will you use to describe the action?

Setting

- ▷ Where will the story take place?
- ▷ What will the setting be like?
- ▷ Have you got a picture of the setting in your mind?
- ▷ When will the story take place? (past, present, future)
- ▷ What words will you use to describe the setting?

Characterisation

- ▷ Who/what are the main characters?
- ▷ What do they look like?
- ▷ What words would you use to describe each one's appearance?
- ▷ How would you describe the nature of each character?

Structure

- ▷ How are you going to begin your story?
- ▷ What will be your lead sentence?

▷ What is the problem in your story?

▷ How is this situation going to be resolved?

▷ How will you end your story?

- Provide children with strategies for planning for narrative writing. For example, before the children start writing they can:

  ▷ Prepare a story map (pictorial representation) to plot the actions and settings of each event in the story.

  ▷ Make a story outline (written form) that roughs out the events and settings of the story.

  ▷ Draw up a character profile on which they add appropriate descriptors for each of the characters in their story.

  ▷ Make a cartoon strip to sequence the events in the story.

  ▷ Chart the type of speech they will write for each character if dialogue is to be used.

  ▷ Tell their planned story to a partner to help them clarify their ideas.

  ▷ Use the above questions for plot, setting and characterisation to help them focus on these elements of their story.

- Model oral story-telling to the children. For example:

  ▷ Instead of always reading to the children rehearse your story-telling skills and then present some stories orally.

  ▷ Employ the services of professional story-tellers to entertain as well as demonstrate the art of story-telling to the children.

  ▷ Ask parents, fellow teachers, members of the community etc. to visit and participate in story-telling sessions.

- Provide plenty of opportunities for the children to practise their oral story-telling skills. For example:

  ▷ Conduct a regular time for story-telling by the children.

  ▷ During Show and Tell time encourage them to present their news in a narrative form instead of the usual personal recount style.

  ▷ A story 'buddy' system could be set up with the older children in the school conducting oral story-telling with younger children. (A Cross-Age Tutoring activity.)

- Provide opportunities for the children to experiment with the use of dialogue in narratives. For example:

  ▷ Provide a situation and ask children to write in dialogue form what each of the characters would say in the situation.

  ▷ The children draw original characters and provide a typical piece of speech.

  ▷ Describe a situation and list the potential characters and ask the children to write what each would say (for example, an old person, a teenager, a teacher, a small child etc.).

  ▷ Provide photos, drawings and illustrations from magazines that show two or more people in a situation. The children add dialogue that they think is appropriate to the picture.

- Make some of the jointly constructed original narratives into big books. Discuss the publishing decisions that need to be made after the text has been written. For example:
  ▷ the size and shape of the big book
  ▷ the amount of text to each page (also consider the size and type of print to be used)
  ▷ the use of illustrations—the placement, type, importance to the text etc.
  ▷ the design of and the information to be included on the cover and title page
  ▷ the importance and design of the end papers
  ▷ the placement and type of blurb and author information.

General activities with narrative texts

The following activities are designed to help children become familiar with the structure of narrative texts and to develop the skills of reading, writing and understanding narratives. Each activity has been chosen because it focuses on either the structure of, characterisation in, or the writing strategies required for narratives. These activities are most effective if first used orally and then used in written form. The activities marked with an asterisk (*) can also be used with factual texts and are explained in greater detail on pages 26 and 27 of this book.

1 Story starter cards

A series of cards is made for each of these story elements: character, setting and situation. The children are arranged in groups of three. The group selects one card from each category and jointly composes a narrative that includes the information on their cards.

2 Picture writing

The children are given a photo, picture or a series of pictures related to the same event and they must write a narrative using the content of the picture as the basis of the story.

3 Writing a parody

The children take a well known story and write it with changes to some or all of the story elements. For example, changes to the characters, setting, complication, resolution, time etc.

4 Finish the story

The teacher begins an original or well known narrative and the children complete it either orally or in a written form.

5 Add a bit stories

An original or familiar story is begun and the children take turns to add to it. This can be an oral or written activity.

6 Writing from another point of view

The children retell a well known story from a character's point of view. For example retell 'Red Riding Hood' from the wolf's, Red Riding Hood's, or the Grandmother's point of view.

7 Pattern writing

Read a story that has repetitive language or a strong pattern to the language. The children write their own text using the pattern. *Who Sank the Boat?* by Pamela Allen and *Brown Bear, Brown Bear, What Do You See?* by B. Martin provide good structures for pattern writing.

8 Story ladders

Provide a framework or outline of a well known narrative and the children complete it to make a coherent retelling of the story. This procedure can also be used for original stories. For example, based on 'The Hare And The Tortoise':

> *The hare and the tortoise decided . . .*
> *The hare was sure that . . .*
> *When the starter's whistle blew . . .*
> *After a while the hare became tired and . . .*

9 Prediction activities

This activity can be used in different ways. For example:
Before reading:
- From the blurb, cover or flicking through the book predict the setting, characters, plot etc.
- The children predict the problems the character may encounter.

During reading:
- Read part of the story and children predict what will happen next.
- Throughout the story the children are asked to predict how the story will end. As the story progresses they can alter their predictions.

10 Antonym substitution

The children rewrite a known story and substitute antonyms for one or all of the following—the adjectives, the adverbs or the verbs. For example—*Replace the words in bold with their antonyms. The prince was a* **tall, dark, handsome** *man. His smile was* **warm** *and* **friendly.** *Cinderella, her* **long, fair** *hair framing her* **pretty** *face, looked* **beautiful** *in her* **pale** *blue dress.*

11 Add the text

The children provide the storyline for wordless picture books. For example Jan Ormerod's wordless books *Moonlight* and *Sunshine* are appropriate for this activity.

12 Build a character

These activities help the children develop better characterisation for their narratives. For example:

- The children draw an original character and then write detailed descriptions of this character.
- A character from a familiar story is chosen and a detailed description is formed.
- Before the children add characters to their own stories they draw and note the features of the character they wish to include in their descriptions.

13 Change the character

The children retell a known story but substitute different characteristics for a selected character. For example:

- Retell 'Red Riding Hood' with the wolf as a kindly helpful character.
- Retell the story of Snow White with the dwarfs being unhelpful and mean.

14 Guess the character

The children work in pairs with one partner writing a detailed description of a familiar character without mentioning the title of the story from which the character is drawn. It must be written well enough for the partner to make an informed guess as to the name of the character.

15 Interview the characters

The children are arranged in pairs and they select one partner to be a character from a familiar story and the other partner to be a reporter. The reporter asks the character questions related to the events in the story and the character provides the answers. Together the pairs can write up the interview as a newspaper article.

16 Character recounts

A familiar story is retold as a series of events from one of the character's point of view. For example:

- The wolf tells what happened in the story 'The Three Little Pigs' or one of the pigs tells what happened.
- The events in 'Goldilocks and the Three Bears' are told by Goldilocks or Baby Bear.

17 Character journal writing

The children select a character from a story they have read and proceed to create a journal in which they record the events and incidents the character experienced in the story.

18 Jumbled stories

The children write an original narrative using characters from well known stories. For example:

- Select a character from a familiar story to be the main character of their original story.
- Combine characters taken from one or more familiar stories to create an original story.
- Select all the characters from a familiar story and create a new story that includes them.

19 Add the complication

The children are given the characters and setting for a story and they think of the complication that could involve these characters and the setting.

20 Change the form

Write the narrative in a different form, ensuring that the appropriate devices are included. For example:

- Rewrite a story as a radio play and include those devices that will enable it to appeal to the listener's imagination.
- Create a video script and accompanying shooting script for a story. Rely on the visual, sound and movement aspects of the script.
- Write a stage play for a story. Add the appropriate stage directions etc.

- Create a puppet play for a story. Add sufficient dialogue for the story to be understood.
- Use one of the children's recounts from show and tell sessions and have them write this as a narrative.
- Write a familiar story in recount form in which the events are described in sequence from one of the character's point of view.

21 Story maps

- The teacher reads a narrative to the children and they provide a map to show, in sequence, the places mentioned in the story. They must show all the details mentioned about each place.
- Provide a story map, based on an original or familiar story and the children provide the narrative.
- The children, as part of their planning for writing, draw a story map to help them clarify their thoughts as to the content of their narrative.

22 Wacky tales

After the teacher has provided details of the characters to be used in an original narrative, each group or group member is given the task of writing either an introduction (orientation), complication (conflict or situation), and resolution (ending). They write these sections independently of one another and at the end of the writing period combine the sections and share the narrative.

23 What's the resolution?

The teacher and children jointly create characters and a complication or problem to be used in an original story. The children, in groups, write a suitable resolution or ending for the story. They share the different resolutions they created.

24 Solve the problem

The children are given a problem involving a familiar book character and they have to write a solution to the problem. For example, Cinderella *wants advice on how to gain an invitation to the ball*. The children write imaginative solutions for her problem.

25 Narrative sort

Sections of a narrative are written on separate pieces of card and distributed to a group of children. Each child must read their section then find and sequence the other pieces that go together to make their particular narrative.

26 Story timelines

The children draw a line that indicates the sequence of events in the narrative.

27 Letter writing

The children create letters from one character to another in a familiar story. For example, they write a letter that the tortoise, after winning the race, may have written to the hare in 'The Hare and the Tortoise'.

28 News report

The children read a narrative and then create a news item about one of the events in the story. They must write it in the style of a news report so modelling of this style of writing will be required.

News reports: another form of writing that needs to be modelled.

Sharing fiction books they have read helps the children understand the many forms of fiction writing.

29 *Readers' circle

The children bring to the circle fiction books they have read and that they wish to share with the group members.

30 *Authors' circle

The children bring to this circle any narratives they have written and wish to share with the group members.

31 *Partner reading and writing activities

For example:
- The children may jointly construct a narrative after co-operatively planning for the writing of it.
- The partners take turns in writing sections of the narrative. One writes a part of the narrative and stops and the other (without any collaboration with the partner) must continue writing so that the story makes sense. They continue taking turns to do this until the story is finished to both partners' satisfaction.

32 *Retell procedure

- The teacher reads a story to the children and they retell it orally.
- As above but the children write a retelling.
- The children read a story and orally retell it.
- As above but the children write a retelling.

Assessment and evaluation of fiction writing

This is a suggested summary of aspects you may wish to use for your own particular evaluation needs. They may help you to set specific objectives for this aspect of your language programme. The selection of objectives will be dependent on the language development of the children you teach. Does the student attempt to include the main elements of narratives in his or her own stories? Is the student able to:
- recognise the different types of fiction?
- plan for narrative writing?
- write interesting first sentences and lead paragraphs?
- use descriptive writing to establish plausible characterisation?
- write satisfactory conclusions?
- use direct speech to build up interesting narratives?
- write events in sequence?
- write cohesive, well sequenced narratives?

TRADITIONAL FICTION

▼

Description

Traditional fiction refers to those texts that originated in the oral form and have been told and retold through the generations until finally they have been recorded in the written narrative form. They consist of the basic structure of orientation, complication and resolution.

Some forms of traditional narratives are:

- folk-tales/fairy-tales (these terms can be interchanged)
- fables
- myths and legends

Learning experiences for folk-tales and fairy-tales

- Discuss with the children the oral origin of folk-tales.
- Discuss the structure of folk-tales. For example:
  - ▷ usually have a simple plot
  - ▷ short, fast moving stories
  - ▷ the characters aren't described in detail
  - ▷ the folk-tales sound as if they are being told to the reader
  - ▷ there is often use of repetition of either words, phrases, situations etc.
  - ▷ there is often a theme or message written into the plot
  - ▷ the introduction is usually very brief and brisk.

- Set up a display of folk-tales. For example:
  - ▷ folk-tales from a selected country
  - ▷ folk-tales from a variety of countries
  - ▷ particular forms of folk-tales (animal tales, cumulative tales, fairy-tales, tales about fools, beasts, explanations etc.).
- Discuss the use of magic in folk-tales (fairy-tales).
- Include the study of folk-tales in the study of other countries.
- Present to the children some of the folk-tales in oral form.
- Encourage the children to practise their story telling skills by orally presenting a folk-tale to the class.
- Present as many variations of the same folk-tale as you can.
- Compare the different illustrative styles of the same folk-tale.
- Compare the same folk-tale as told in another country (Cinderella has over 900 versions around the world.*)
- Demonstrate the written retelling of a familiar folk-tale.
- Jointly construct a written retelling of a familiar folk-tale.
- Jointly construct an original tale based around a theme or message included in a familiar folk-tale.
- Use a familiar folk-tale as a 'scaffold' and rewrite it:
  - ▷ to suit another country
  - ▷ using different characters.
- Discuss the difference between traditional and modern fairy-tales. For example:
  - ▷ modern fairy-tales originated in the written form
  - ▷ modern fairy-tales can be accredited to particular authors
  - ▷ traditional fairy-tales had oral origins and no particular authors.
  - ▷ Both traditional and modern fairy-tales reflect the battles between good and evil in which good always wins.
- Read as many modern fairy-tales to the children as possible.
- Set up a display of fairy-tales in one of the following ways:
  - ▷ fairy-tales by the one author (Hans Christian Andersen, Oscar Wilde, Jane Yolen etc.)
  - ▷ the same fairy-tale illustrated by different illustrators
  - ▷ books of collections of modern fairy-tales
  - ▷ modern and traditional fairy-tales
  - ▷ fairy-tales with the same type of characters, settings, plots, elements of magic etc.
  - ▷ any parodies of fairy-tales.
- Model the written retelling of a modern fairy-tale.
- Jointly construct an original fairy-tale using a contemporary setting and characters.
- Discuss the plot, setting and characters in familiar modern fairy-tales using the guiding questions related to narratives.

• • • • • • • • • • • • • • •
* Anne Hanzl, *East of the Sun, West of the Moon.*

Exploring traditional narratives: folk-tales—a sample unit

This sample unit includes ideas for modelling sessions to be used within a language lesson. The modelling time would take no more than fifteen to twenty minutes. The suggestions for further activities would take extra time and may or may not be added to the modelling session time. They may be conducted in separate sessions with individual children, groups or the whole class.

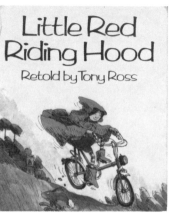

Demonstration books:

Red Riding Hood by Brenda Parkes (Oxford University Press, 1989) also available in big book format.

Little Red Riding Hood by Tony Ross (Hutchinson Group (Australia) Pty Ltd, 1978). This book is not in big book format. It is not essential for the children to see the text, if you do not have multiple copies of the book, but as you are reading the story to them ensure that they are able to look at the illustrations on each page.

Session One

> **Focus**—Introduction to the term 'folk-tales' and the oral retelling of Red Riding Hood.

- Talk about the term 'folk-tales' and how these began in the oral form.
- List the characters in Red Riding Hood and their features.
- Ask the children to tell you the story of Red Riding Hood.
- As the children tell the story ask if any of them disagree with the content being told. Why might this happen?

Further activities

- Find as many different versions of Red Riding Hood as you can.
- Build a story map of the original version of the story.
- Construct character profiles for each of the characters in the story.

Session Two

> **Focus**—The changes in the retelling of Red Riding Hood over the period of time for various reasons.

- Look at the cover of the Brenda Parkes version of Red Riding Hood and ask the children to tell you if it will be as they remember the story. Why?
- Read *Red Riding Hood* by Brenda Parkes.
- Note the differences between the original and this retelling.
- Discuss why these changes may have been included.
- Note how the illustrations have added extra information to the text.

Extension activity

- The children orally retell the Brenda Parkes version of Red Riding Hood.

Session Three

> **Focus** — The introduction to the term 'parody'

- Read Tony Ross's *Little Red Riding Hood*.
- Note the differences in his version of the story.
- Introduce the children to the term 'parody' and what it means.
- List all the examples of this in Tony Ross's *Little Red Riding Hood*.

Extension activity

- Collect, display and read to the children other folk- and fairy-tales that are parodies of the original.

Session Four

> **Focus** — The planning for and the oral telling of another parody of Red Riding Hood

- Decide to change one of these aspects of the story of Red Riding Hood:
  - ▷ the setting
  - ▷ the nature of all or some of the characters
  - ▷ the ending of the story
  - ▷ parts of the plot.
- Jointly construct an oral parody of Red Riding Hood which includes one of the above changes.

Further activities

- In groups the children can create further oral parodies of Red Riding Hood which include several of the above suggestions for change.

- In groups make up oral parodies of other folk-tales or fairy-tales. Present them to the class.

Group preparation and presentation of oral parodies of folk-tales provides further exploration of writing forms.

Session Five

Focus — The planning for and the writing of a draft of a parody

- Use one of the oral parodies as a basis of the draft and demonstrate the planning for and the drafting of a parody.

Further activities

- The children in groups can select a familiar folk-tale and write their own parody of it. These written parodies can be read to the class.
- A class-book can be made of the children's parodies. For example:
  ▷ 'Our Versions Of Red Riding Hood'
  ▷ 'Our Twisted Folk-tales'
  ▷ 'Cinderella As It Was Never Intended'.

Books to further explore folk-tales and fairy-tales with the children

BB   This indicates that a book is also available in big book format.

Alexiou, Petro. *Misokolaki*. Harcourt Brace Jovanovich, 1989. **BB**

Andersen, Hans Christian. *The Tinderbox*. Illustrated by Warwick Hutton, Margaret McElderry Books, 1988.

Barber, Martha. *The Funny Old Man and the Funny Old Woman*. Bookshelf, Martin Educational, 1987. **BB**

Bolton, Fay. *The Greedy Goat*. Martin Educational, Bookshelf Series, 1986. **BB**

Collins, Michael, (ed.). *Folk Tales From Asia*. Bookshelf, Martin Educational, 1987.

dePaola, Tomie. *The Magic Pasta Pot*. Anderson, 1984.

French, Fiona. *Snow White in New York*. Oxford University Press, 1989.

Hanzl, Ann. *Silly Willy*. Bookshelf, Martin Educational, 1986. **BB**

Haviland, Virginia. *Favourite Fairy Tales told in Denmark*. Little Brown, 1971.

Kent, Jack. *The Fat Cat*. Penguin, 1974.

Klein, R. *Brock and the Dragon*. Hodder & Stoughton, 1984.

Morimoto, Junko. *A Piece of Straw*. Collins, 1985.

Morimoto, Junko. *The White Crane*. Collins, 1983.

Mosel, Arlene. *Tikki Tikki Tembo*. Holt, 1968.

Munsch, N. *The Paper Bag Princess*. Ashton Scholastic, 1989. **BB**

O'Toole, Mary. *Stone Soup*. Southern Cross Series, Macmillan, 1987. **BB**

Learning experiences for fables

- Discuss the origin of fables.
  - ▷ Aesop's Fables (Greek origin)
  - ▷ La Fontaine (French origin)
- Collect information on Aesop and La Fontaine.
- Discuss the structure of fables:
  - ▷ Brief tales written to convey a message or to teach a lesson.
  - ▷ Most use animal characters that have human traits.
  - ▷ The plot is usually simple and based on one event.
- Read as many versions of the same fable and discuss the features of each.
- Set up a collection of fables. For example:
  - ▷ same fable different presentation
  - ▷ artists' impressions of fables
  - ▷ same message or moral in different fables
  - ▷ fables from same source (La Fontaine, Aesop, modern fables).
- Read as many fables to the children as possible.
- Compare the modern versions of fables with the traditional versions.
- Model the written retelling of a familiar fable.
- List several morals as they are revealed in fables.
- Select a particular moral and create an original fable to emphasise this message. This can be done in the following ways:
  - ▷ teacher modelling own fable writing
  - ▷ jointly constructing an original fable
  - ▷ co-operative group work to write an original fable
  - ▷ individual writing of an original fable.

- Read a selection of fables and ask the children to find the message in each and express the message in their own words.
- List some common sayings or proverbs and have the children write a fable that will demonstrate one of these. For example: write a fable that will include the message 'co-operation is better than conflict'.
- Read some of Leo Lionni's modern fables and discuss the message conveyed in each.

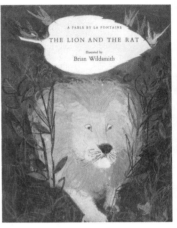

Exploring traditional narratives: fables—a sample unit

This sample unit includes ideas for modelling sessions to be used within a language lesson. The modelling time would take no more than fifteen to twenty minutes. The suggestions for further activities would take extra time and may or may not be added to the modelling session time. They may be conducted in separate sessions with individual children, groups or the whole class.

Demonstration books:

The Lion and the Rat by Brian Wildsmith (Oxford University Press, 1963).

The Hare and the Tortoise by Brian Wildsmith (Oxford University Press, 1966).

The Richman and the Shoe-maker by Brian Wildsmith (Oxford University Press, 1965).

The Miller, the Boy and the Donkey by Brian Wildsmith (Oxford University Press, 1969).

These books are not in big book format. It is not essential for the children to see the text but as you are reading the fables to them ensure that they are able to look at the illustrations on each page.

Fables by Arnold Lobel (Harper and Row, 1980).

This book is not in big book format. It is not essential for the children to see all of the text but as you are reading the fables to them ensure that they are able to look at the illustrations on each page and are able to read the moral at the end of fable. You may need to write the morals in large print so the children can see them clearly.

Session One

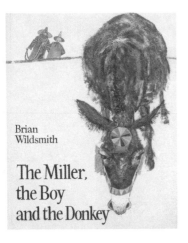

> **Focus**—Introduction to fables, their purpose and structure

- Read to the children *The Lion and the Rat* and *The Hare and the Tortoise*.
- Discuss the message from each fable. Introduce the term 'moral'.
- Ask the children the following:
  - ▷ What are the main characters in these fables?
  - ▷ Why do you think animals are used to help teach the message in each fable?
  - ▷ What did you notice about the style of writing in each of these fables?
  - ▷ Why are the illustrations important in each of these fables?
  - ▷ What is the same/different about each of these fables?

Further activities

- Find out information on La Fontaine and make a class chart with facts about him.
- Collect fables by La Fontaine.
- Collect and read to the children further fables and discuss the moral of each one.

Session Two

> **Focus**—Fables that don't have animals as central characters

- Read *The Miller, the Boy and the Donkey* and *The Rich Man and the Shoe-maker* to the children.
- At the end of each fable ask:
  - ▷ What is the moral of this fable?
  - ▷ What did La Fontaine use to convey this moral?
  - ▷ Who/what are the main characters?

Further activities

- Ask the children to find examples from their experiences that reflect the messages in the above fables.
- Using one of the above experiences have the children in groups orally form it into a fable.
- Find other fables that don't use animals as the main characters.

Session Three

> **Focus**—Modern fables using animal characters

- Read and share with the children several of Lobel's fables. Do not let the children see the moral written at the end of each fable.
- After each reading have the children suggest the moral that was the basis of the fable. Ask them to give reasons for their choice of moral. Uncover the moral to see if they were correct.
- Alternatively, cover the text of a selected Lobel fable except for the moral at the conclusion of the fable. Allow the children to read the moral, study the illustration and then suggest an appropriate fable to go with these two clues.

Session Four

> **Focus**—Creating fables for common sayings

- Provide a list of some common proverbs or sayings. For example:
  - ▷ Co-operation is better than conflict.
  - ▷ Two heads are better than one.
  - ▷ Where there's a will there's a way.
  - ▷ One good turn deserves another etc.

  Some proverbs and colloquialisms are good sources of ideas for creating fables with a meaningful message.
- Ask the children to think of a familiar story or fable that demonstrates any of these.
- Select one of these sayings and model the planning for writing of a fable:
  - ▷ select appropriate animal characters
  - ▷ draw a map to show the sequence of events
  - ▷ ensure that the moral will be stated at the conclusion of the original fable.

Session Five

> **Focus**—The writing of an original fable

- Jointly construct a fable using the plan created in the previous session.
- As the text is being constructed constantly demonstrate the work of a writer. For example:
  - ▷ rereading and reworking sections

▷ selecting more appropriate vocabulary
▷ reordering parts of the fable so the events are in logical sequence
▷ making sure the text is not too long.

Further activities

- The above fable may be completed in published form.
- The children may wish to write their own fable to demonstrate a particular moral.
- The children may wish to rewrite a familiar fable with a different focus. For example:
  ▷ Involving human characters and not animals. (The moral involved in 'The Lion and the Mouse' woven into a story line about a school bully and a shy little schoolboy.)

Books to further explore fables with the children

BB   This indicates that a book is also available in big book format.

Aesop's Fables. Illustrated by Heidi Holder. Macmillan, 1981.
Biro, Val. *Fables from Aesop*. Ginn and Company, 1984.
Lionni, Leo. *It's Mine*. Anderson Press, 1986.
Lionni, Leo. *Cornelius*. Anderson Press, 1983.
Ross, Tony. *Foxy Fables*, Puffin, 1986.
Seuss, Dr. *Sneetches*. Collins, 1965.
The Boy who Cried Wolf—An Aesop Fable. Retold by Mary O'Toole. Macmillan, 1987. **BB**
The Hare and the Tortoise. Retold by Caroline Castle. Dial Books For Young Children, 1985.
Wildsmith, Brian. *The North Wind and the Sun*. Oxford University Press, 1964.

Fables in play form
Leask, Jeffrey. *Nowhere Boy—A Musical Fable*. Martin Educational, 1988.

Learning experiences for myths and legends

- Discuss the origin of myths:
  ▷ myths began with primitive man
  ▷ they were used to explain the origin of things
  ▷ they included gods to explain creation of things.

- Discuss the different types of myths:
  - ▷ creation myths
  - ▷ myths that explain natural phenomena
  - ▷ myths about heroes (called legends).
- Read to the children as many myths as possible.
- Model the written retelling of a familiar myth.
- Collect and read myths from a particular country (ancient Greece, Rome, ancient Scandinavia etc.).
- Read Greek myths and build up a chart of the gods and goddesses included in the stories and add the characteristics of each.
- Jointly construct a myth using some of the gods or goddesses listed previously.
- Model the writing of an original myth to explain the creation of some natural phenomena.
- Read a selection of Aboriginal myths and legends to the children.
- Note the language used to introduce Aboriginal myths and legends (the reference to the Dreamtime).
- Discuss what each Aboriginal legend attempts to explain.
- Jointly construct a written retelling of an Aboriginal myth or legend.
- Jointly construct a myth in the style of Australian Aboriginal or American Indian myths to explain the appearance or characteristics of animals, plants, birds or any natural phenomena:
  - ▷ how the owl got his huge eyes
  - ▷ why buffalo move in herds
  - ▷ why thunder accompanies lightning.

Exploring traditional narrative: myths and legends—a sample unit

This sample unit includes ideas for modelling sessions to be used within a language lesson. The modelling time would take no more than fifteen to twenty minutes. The suggestions for further activities would take extra time and may or may not be added to the modelling session time. They may be conducted in separate sessions with individual children, groups or the whole class.

Demonstration books:

Pheasant and Kingfisher by Catherine Berndt, Bookshelf, Martin Educational, 1987 (available in big book format).

The Girl Who Loved Wild Horses by Paul Goble, Aladdin Books, Macmillan, 1978.

Session One

> **Focus**—Introduction to *Pheasant and Kingfisher* and Aboriginal legends

- Read *Pheasant and Kingfisher* to page 10, then stop and ask the children what they think the ending of the story will be.
- Complete the story and allow time for the children to discuss their impressions and predictions of how the story would end. Ask:
  - ▷ What was this story trying to explain?
  - ▷ How would this story have originated? Why?

Further activities

- Locate the place of the story.
- Set up displays of Aboriginal myths and legends.
- Collect pictures of Aboriginal art to display around the room.
- Text analysis: provide headings for each page of the text.

Session Two

> **Focus**—Introduction to *The Girl Who Loved Wild Horses* and American Indian myths and legends

- Show the cover of the book and ask the children to predict what the story could be about and where they think it's set.
- Read the story to the children.

Further activities

- Set up a display of American Indian myths and legends.
- Compare the artistic styles of Aboriginal and American Indians.

Session Three

> **Focus**—The structure of a myth

- Revisit each of the books and ask the children to examine the differences and similarities between Aboriginal and American Indian myths. Compile a chart recording their comments.

- Ask the children these questions to focus their attention on the structure of myths:
  - ▷ What would have been the original form of these myths?
  - ▷ Why would the authors have wished to record these myths in written form?
  - ▷ What were the myths trying to explain?
  - ▷ What did the authors need to know to be able to record these myths?
  - ▷ How did the authors begin each story?

Further activities

- Compare Aboriginal and American Indian myths with those of another people.
- Build up a display of myths and legends from all over the world and compare the styles.
- Provide guiding questions to help the children compare these myths and legends.

Session Four

> **Focus**—Creating myths to explain phenomena

- Briefly discuss each of the myths read and what they explained.
- Form the children into groups of three and ask them to create an oral explanation in the form of an Aboriginal or American Indian myth for one of the following:
  - ▷ how the mountains/canyons were formed
  - ▷ why the eagle has such good eyesight
  - ▷ why coyotes howl
  - ▷ how the kookaburra got his laugh.

Session five

> **Focus**—The written recording of a myth

- The groups form their oral myth into written form, being careful to include:
  - ▷ the traditional beginning
  - ▷ Australian Aboriginal/American Indian names where possible
  - ▷ Australian Aboriginal/American Indian place names
  - ▷ an ending that explains what the myth was describing.
- These are shared with the rest of the class.

Further activities

- Form a class-book of the myths and legends created by the groups.
- The groups can dramatise their myths and legends.

Books to further explore myths and legends with the children

Bates, Daisy. *Tales Told to Kabbarli*. Retold by Barbara Ker Wilson, Crown, 1972.
Berndt, Catherine. *When the World was New*. Bookshelf, Martin Educational, 1988.
Creation Myths. Retold by Maureen Stewart, Southern Cross Series, Macmillan, 1987.
Binner, Cynthia & Binner, William. *Song to Demeter*. Julia MacRae, 1987.
Crossley-Holland, Kevin. *Norse Myths*. Penguin, 1982.
Goble, Paul. *Buffalo Woman*. Aladdin Books, Macmillan, 1986.
Green, Roger L. *Tales of Greek Heroes*. Penguin, 1970.
Hanzl, Anne, (Reteller). *Thor Outwits the Giants*. Bookshelf, Martin Educational, 1989.
Homer. *The Odyssey*. Kingfisher, 1987.
Lofts, Pamela. *Dunbi The Owl*. Ashton Scholastic, 1983.
Lofts, Pamela. *How the Birds got their Colours*. Ashton Scholastic, 1984.
Maralngura, N. et al. *Djugurba Tales from the Spirit Time*. Australian National University Press, 1974.
Roughsey, Dick. *The Rainbow Serpent*. Collins Fontana, 1975.
Tresize, Percy. *Banana Bird and the Snake Men*. Collins, 1980.
Tresize, P. & Roughsey, D. *Turramulli the Great Quinkin*. Collins, 1982.
Tresize, Percy. *The Magic Firesticks*. Collins, 1980.
Usher, Kerry. *Heroes, Gods and Emperors from Roman Mythology*. P. Lowe, 1983.
Walker, Kath. *Father Sky Mother Earth*. Jacaranda, 1985.

Assessment and evaluation of traditional narrative writing

This is a suggested summary of aspects you may wish to use for your own particular evaluation needs. They may help you to set specific objectives for your language programme. The selection of objectives will be dependent on the language development of the children you teach. Does the student attempt to write an original narrative in any of the traditional forms? Is the student able to:

- distinguish between folk-tales, myths and fables?
- orally retell a traditional tale?
- write a retelling of a traditional narrative?
- discuss the origin of traditional narratives?

MODERN FICTION

▼

Description

Modern fiction refers to those texts that originated in the written form and are the result of a creative imagination. The authors employ realistic or fanciful devices in their writing to reflect some aspect of life or life's problems and the plots can be set in the past, present or future. This section is concerned with modern narratives which comprise an orientation, complication and resolution. The study of poetry in its many forms is not within the scope of this book.

This section includes:
- contemporary realistic narratives (These texts have been defined as '. . . imaginative writing which reflects life as it was lived in the past or could be lived today'.*)
- modern fantasy (These texts are written as a result of a creative and fanciful imagination and present characters, settings or situations within a web of wonder or magic. Modern fantasy includes modern fairy-tales and science fiction.)

Learning experiences for contemporary realistic narratives

- Discuss the characteristics of this writing form. For example:
  ▷ has a well developed plot, characterisation and setting
  ▷ written to include orientation, complication and resolution

* Charlotte Huck, *Children's Literature in the Elementary School*, p. 394.

▷ written to involve the reader in a good story that depicts life as it was lived or is lived today

▷ usually the story is based on the writer's interests, experiences, problems or feelings

▷ a real life problem or issue may be explored by the writer

▷ the texts may have a long story line

▷ contemporary realistic narratives can be represented in the following forms:
  - animal stories
  - humorous stories
  - sports stories
  - mysteries
  - historical fiction.

- Demonstrate how some picture story-books can present the events and problems faced in the past or present with the use of well constructed text and detailed illustrations that complement the text.

- Read to the children as many forms of contemporary realistic fiction as possible. For example:

  ▷ animal stories that help the children explore their own relationships and attitudes toward animals

  ▷ humorous stories that amuse the children while exploring the problems of the main characters

  ▷ mysteries that capitalise on the children's interests and are well written according to all the criteria of good narratives.

- Select books according to the issue or problem you wish to explore with the children (divorce, survival, friendships, conflict etc.).

- Collect books on the same issue and allow the children to browse, select and read as desired. For example, the issue may be 'the aged' so fiction and factual books are selected on the basis of the subject:

  ▷ *Wilfred Gordon McDonald Partridge* by Mem Fox

  ▷ *After the Goatman* by Betsy Byars

  ▷ *Nana Upstairs and Nana Downstairs* by Tomie de Paola

  ▷ *Penny Pollard's Diary* by Robin Klein

  ▷ *How Does It Feel To Be Old?* by Norma Farber.

- Select an issue and have the children write their thoughts on it (for example, bullies at school, children's fears, a new baby in the family, etc.).

- Use the children's thoughts on issues and jointly construct a narrative text that reflects these.

- Model the planning for and writing of narratives and relate this to the children's own writing.

- When reading books of this type to the children relate the author's writing process back to the children's own writing by asking the following:

  ▷ Why do you think the author wrote this book?

▷ Where do you think the author got the idea for the book?

▷ How do you think the author planned for the writing of this book? (The use of story maps, Character Profiles, research, drafting etc.)

Exploring contemporary realistic narratives—a sample unit

This sample unit includes ideas for modelling sessions to be used within a language lesson. The modelling time would take no more than fifteen to twenty minutes. The suggestions for further activities would take extra time and may or may not be added to the modelling session time. They may be conducted in separate sessions by individuals, groups or the whole class.

Demonstration book:

Wilfrid Gordon McDonald Partridge by Mem Fox (Omnibus, 1984).

Wilfrid Gordon McDonald Partridge
Written by Mem Fox   Illustrated by Julie Vivas

Session One

> **Focus**—The introduction to the book and the structure of a picture story-book narrative

- Show the children the cover of the book and ask them to predict the contents of the book. They must give reasons for their prediction.
- Read the story to the children and allow time for the children to study the illustrations.
- Focus on the orientation of the story (characters, setting, and time of story) by asking:
  ▷ What is the setting of the story?
  ▷ Who are the main characters?
  ▷ When do you think this story is set? Why?
- Focus on the complication or main situation of the story by asking:
  ▷ What is the main event that the main character is involved in?
- Focus on the resolution (ending) by asking:
  ▷ What happens at the end of the story?
- Focus on the theme of the book by asking:
  ▷ What do you think the author is trying to describe or explain in this story?

Further activities

- Set up a class display of books about the elderly. Include fiction and factual books.
- Read to the children a selection of books related to this theme and ask them the above questions which focus on the structure of narratives.
- The children can interview their parents and grandparents and collect some of their childhood memories to write up at a later date.
- Set up separate charts on which the children can write their favourite childhood memories and those of their parents and their grandparents. Compare each of these with their own memories chart.

Session Two

> **Focus**—The work of an author when creating characters for a narrative. Relating this to the children's own writing process.

- Reread the book and ask the children to select words that would describe Wilfrid Gordon and Miss Nancy.
- Build up a Character Profile of each of these characters.
- Focus on the author's work when creating the characters by asking the children:
  - ▷ What did Mem Fox need to know about these characters before writing?
  - ▷ How may Mem Fox have found out about the type of characters?
  - ▷ How might she have planned to write about them?
- Link the responses to the children's own writing so they can relate the author's work to their own writing process.

Further activities

- Select pictures of elderly people and in groups the children can build up Character Profiles for each of these.
- Each child may bring to school a photo of a grandparent and create a character profile and subsequent written description of them.
- Read *Sophie*, also by Mem Fox, and discuss:
  - ▷ the similarity of theme to the above book
  - ▷ the attitudes or values of Mem Fox that are revealed in the content of both books
  - ▷ how Mem Fox may have got the ideas for each of the books
  - ▷ the importance of the illustrations in this book in adding the extra information the text doesn't provide.

Session Three

Focus—The difference between recounts and narratives

- Share some of the earliest or funniest memories that the children have collected. Most of these will be recounts, which should consist of:
  - ▷ a simple retelling of an event that someone has been involved in
  - ▷ a very brief statement of time, place, setting and participants in the event
  - ▷ a well sequenced description of happenings of the recount.
- Select one of these memories and model the oral structuring of this from a recount to a narrative.
- Discuss the difference between the two oral presentations of the same memory. For example:
  - ▷ The narrative relies on the developing of interesting character and setting descriptions.
  - ▷ The plot is based around a situation or complication in the story.
  - ▷ The ending deals with the complication in the story.
  - ▷ It uses more descriptive words and action words than the recount.

Extension activity

- In groups of three the children use the listed memories as a stimulus event to create an oral narrative.

Group retelling of their oral narrative helps the children rehearse for the written activity.

Session Four

Focus—Modelling the planning for a written narrative

- Tell the children that you are going to jointly construct a narrative suitable for a short picture story-book. It is to be based on one of the memories collected by the children.
- Decide on the plot of the story and jointly construct a story map or story outline. Ensure that the events to be included in the story are properly sequenced.
- Construct a Character Profile for each of the characters to be included in the narrative.

Extension activity

- Read further narratives and have the children compile Character Profiles or story maps for these.

Session Five

Focus — The drafting of a written narrative

- Review the planning for narrative writing that was compiled in the previous session and then jointly construct a first draft of the text in front of the children.
- Ensure that:
  ▷ It is not written as a recount.
  ▷ The setting, characters and time of the story are established early in the narrative.
  ▷ There is only one main event in the story. The conclusion is interesting and fitting.

Extension activity

- Reread the narrative that was jointly constructed in the previous session and rework the sections in front of the children taking care to model writer-like behaviours.
  For example:
  ▷ rereading and altering as required
  ▷ reorganising or reworking sections
  ▷ inserting extra or better words or information
  ▷ attending to punctuation and spelling
  ▷ planning for the publishing of the final draft.

Books to further explore contemporary realistic narratives with the children

BB This indicates that a book is also available in big book format.

Baillie, Alan. *Little Brother*. Nelson, 1985. (refugees)
Blume, Judy. *It's not the End of the World*. Pan, 1988. (divorce)
Blume, Judy. *Tales of a Fourth Grade Nothing*. Piccolo, 1981. (family)
Bolton, Barbara. *Edward Wilkins and his Friend Gwendoline*. Golden Press, 1985. (the elderly)
Brighton, Catherine. *Cathy's Story*. Evans Brothers, 1980. (the elderly)
Catterwell, Thelma. *Sebastian Lives in a Hat*. Omnibus, 1989.
Cleary, Beverley. *Dear Mr Henshaw*. Julia MacRae Books, 1983. (divorce)
Farber, Norma. *How Does It Feel To Be Old?* Unicorn Book, E. P. Dutton, 1979.
Fox, Mem. *Sophie*. Drakeford, 1989. (the elderly)
French, Simon. *All We Know*. Angus and Robertson, 1986. (friendship)
Gand, Stephen. *Lights Out*. Jacaranda Press, 1988. (the elderly) **BB**
Graham, Amanda. *Arthur*. Magic Bean, Era Publications, 1988.
Holm, Anne. *I am David*. Methuen, 1965. (refugees)

Klein, Robin. *Boss of the Pool*. Omnibus, 1986. (disabilities)
Klein, Robin. *The Enemies*. Blue Gum, 1986. (friendship)
Klein, Robin. *Hating Alison Ashley*. Puffin, 1984. (friendship)
Klein, Robin. *Penny Pollard's Diary*. Oxford University Press, 1983. (the elderly)
Lester, Alison, *Clive Eats Alligators*. Oxford University Press, 1988. **BB**
MacLeod, Doug. *P'Tik P'Tok*. Southern Cross Series, Macmillan, 1987. (friendship)
Marshall, V. & Tester, B. *Bernard Was A Bikie*. Bookshelf, Martin Educational, 1988. **BB**
McLean, Andrew & Janet. *The Riverboat Crew*. Oxford University Press, 1988.
McLean, Andrew & Janet. *The Steam Train Crew*. Oxford University Press, 1988.
Morris, Johnny, (ed.). *The Faber Book of Animal Stories*. Faber and Faber, 1978.
Nicholls, Bron. *Three Way Street*. Puffin, 1984.
Wheatly, Nadia. *Five Times Dizzy*. Oxford University Press, 1983. (prejudice)

Learning experiences for modern fantasy

- Discuss the characteristics of modern fantasy. For example:
  - ▷ Usually reflects in an imaginative way some aspect of present day living.
  - ▷ The fantasy aspect may be through:
    - i Characters (magic powers to humans, animals or objects, for example in *The Magic Finger* by Roald Dahl)
    - ii the setting (imaginary, strange places)
    - iii the plot (imaginary events that often reflect issues in our society, for example in *The Lorax* by Dr Seuss).
  - ▷ The fantasy is plausible.
- Select examples of modern fantasy and read these to the children (as serial stories if necessary).
- Use modern fantasy as a basis for discussing the ways of creating convincing characterisation.
- Model write a descriptive passage about a familiar character.
- Jointly construct a description for a familiar character.
- Provide opportunities for the children to create descriptions for original characters.
- Compile a class-book of the children's original fantasy writing.
- Rewrite a section of a modern fantasy in another form. For example: rewrite part of *A Bear Called Paddington* by Michael Bond in play form. Discuss the special requirements for play writing.
- Model summary writing at the conclusion of reading a chapter of, or an entire, modern fantasy.
- Build up a serial written retelling as each part of a modern fantasy is read.

Learning experiences for science fiction

- Discuss the characteristics of science fiction. For example:
  ▷ It is based on the possible effects that scientific advances in technology and knowledge could have on mankind, the earth or the universe.
  ▷ The imagination of the author uses the possibilities of science to create the fiction.
  ▷ The structure is the same as other narratives (orientation, complication and resolution).
- Read as many examples of science fiction to the children as possible.
- Focus on the work of a particular science fiction author (L'Engle, Norton, John Christopher, Nicholas Fisk etc.) and find the similarities and differences between each of the books.
- List scientific terms as they are found by the children.
- Discuss some scientific advances and brainstorm the implications of these now and the possibilities if we leave the advancements to the limits of our imagination. For example: robots are used in car manufacturing assembly lines. Children list the intended uses of the robots and the imaginative uses and situations involving robots.

INTENDED USE
To conduct the dangerous, repetitive and boring jobs.
To reduce the number of workers required.
To reduce the costs of car manufacturing.

POSSIBILITIES
Could take over the factory.
Could run out of control.
Could construct weird cars.

- Use ideas listed in the above activity to provide the basis for a jointly constructed science fiction text.
- List undesirable situations in the world today (hole in the ozone layer, sea pollution, droughts, earthquakes, etc.) and have the children brainstorm an imaginative scientific solution to one or each of the problems.
- Model the construction of a science fiction text. Discuss that it has the same structure as any narrative (orientation, complication and resolution). The plot, characters or setting will have a scientific influence.

Exploring modern fantasy— a sample unit

This sample unit includes ideas for modelling sessions to be used within a language lesson. The modelling time would take no more than fifteen to twenty minutes. The suggestions for further activities would take extra time and may or may not be added to the modelling session time. They may be conducted in separate sessions with individual children, groups or the whole class.

Demonstration book:

Felix and Alexander by Terry Denton (Oxford University Press, 1988).

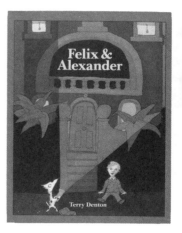

Session One

> **Focus**—Introduction to *Felix and Alexander* and to the term 'fantasy'

- Show the children the title only and ask them to predict what type of book it will be (fiction, narrative). Show them the complete cover to allow them to confirm or alter their predictions.
- Read the book to the children and allow time for them to study the illustrations.
- Ask the children:
  ▷ Could all the events in this story really happen?
  ▷ Why not?
  ▷ Can events in some fiction stories really happen?
  ▷ What has the author used to make this story one that couldn't really happen?
- Introduce the children to the term 'fantasy' if they are not already familiar with it.
- Ask the children the following questions:
  ▷ What did the author use as the main source of fantasy?
  ▷ What parts in this story were fantasy?

Further activities

- The children list all their favourite stories that are fantasies and suggest the source of the fantasy for each of their suggestions (character, setting, situation etc.).

- Set up a display of both modern and traditional fantasy and read a selection these to the children.

Session Two

> **Focus**—The structure of the narrative with emphasis on the setting

- Ask the children to identify the orientation (beginning), problem (middle) and resolution (ending of the story).
- Ask the children to tell you the important parts of the story in sequence.
- Draw a story map or a story line to show these.
- Ask the children:
  - ▷ What was the author trying to tell us in this story?
  - ▷ Where is the story set?
  - ▷ How is the setting depicted in this story?
- Brainstorm adjectives to describe the setting and build up a Setting Profile for the story.

Further activities

- In groups of three the children are to create a new setting for a story they will write about the characters Felix and Alexander later on (beach, country, farm, circus, shopping centre etc.).
- The children draw a new setting. They may talk about the possible story line as they work. They are to write a list of describing words for this new setting and then share these adjectives with another group. The children attempt a descriptive passage to describe this new setting.

Session Three

> **Focus**—Building up Character Profiles

- Note that in the story the characters are not well developed. Discuss the reasons for this.
- Ask the children to suggest ways to develop Alexander's character. List the adjectives they suggest. Concentrate on his description, fears, feelings, habits, favourite toys etc.
- Repeat the process with Felix or create another toy that can have a source of fantasy.

Extension activity

- In groups of three the children can create their own character description for each of the characters. They are to write a descriptive passage for each of the characters.

Session Four

> **Focus**—Creating a problem that will be the basis of a fantasy

- Ask the children the following:
  - ▷ In the book what problem did Terry Denton use as part of the story?
  - ▷ What fears/feelings did Alexander or Felix possibly experience?
- Discuss the fact that even though the book is a fantasy in picture-book format the problem could happen and the feelings aroused are those we can feel.
- Ask the children to list the things they worry about or that can/could cause them problems.
- Select some of these suggested problems and have the children brainstorm solutions that will use some element of fantasy to solve them.

Further activities

- In groups of three the children use the setting and characters they have created to work out a problem that will be the basis of their story.
- They can begin the planning for their story using a story map or a story line etc.
- They may share these plans with other class members.

A group of three students reading as part of the planning exercise for group writing.

Session Five

> **Focus**—Writing a draft of a fantasy

- ◆ Revisit the book and revise how the author may have planned for his writing, for example the process of drawing story maps, telling the story to someone, writing, reading and rewriting. Encourage the children to do this with their own writing.

Further activities

In groups of three the children create a story map for a picture story-book about the characters Felix and Alexander. Write in the features that will add to the fantasy (other characters, an unusual part of the setting, a strange problem or type of illustrations etc.).
- ◆ The children then complete their drafts.
- ◆ They may share their drafts with the remainder of the class.
- ◆ Compile a class-book of the 'Further Fantastic Adventures of Felix and Alexander'.

Books to further explore modern fantasy and science fiction with the children

BB This indicates that a book is also available in big book format.

Burmingham, John. *Mr Gumpy's Outing*. Puffin, 1978.
Bond, Michael. *A Bear Called Paddington*. Fontana, 1972.
Christopher, John. *White Mountains*. Kestrel, 1984.
Coleridge, Ann. *The Friends of Emily Culpepper*. Collins Fontana, 1983.
Condon, Bill. *Wonkyzap and the Time Twister*. Southern Cross Series, Macmillan, 1987. (a play)
Cooper, Susan. *The Dark is Rising*. Puffin, 1976.
Cooper, Susan. *Over Sea, Under Stone*. Penguin, 1984.
Dahl, Roald. *Charlie and the Chocolate Factory*. Puffin, 1985.
Dahl, Roald. *The Magic Finger*. Puffin, 1974.
Dahl, Roald. *The B.F.G.* Puffin, 1984.
Dahl, Roald. *Matilda*. Puffin, 1989.
Dann, Max. *Ernest Pickle's Remarkable Robot*. Oxford University Press, 1984.
Denton, Terry. *Felix and Alexander*. Oxford University Press, 1985. **BB**
Dr Seuss. *The Lorax*. Collins, 1971.
Fisk, Nicholas. *Space Hostages*. Puffin, 1970.
Fisk, Nicholas. *Grinnie*. Puffin, 1975.
Fisk, Nicholas. *A Rag, a Bone and a Hank of Hair*. Puffin, 1982.
Fox, Mem. *Possum Magic*. Omnibus, 1989. **BB**

Freeman, Don. *Corduroy*. Puffin, 1976.
Heide, Florence Parry. *The Shrinking of Treehorn*. Puffin, 1975.
Hunt, Nan. *Junk Eaters*. Southern Cross Series, Macmillan, 1987.
Klein, R. *Thing*. Oxford University Press, 1982.
Klein, R. *Halfway across the Galaxy and Turn Left*. Puffin, 1987.
L'Engle, Madeleine. *A Wrinkle in Time*. Puffin, 1967.
Lindsay, N. *Magic Pudding*. Angus and Robertson, 1975.
Redhead, Janet Slater. *The Big Block of Chocolate*. Ashton Scholastic, 1985.
Rubinstein, Gillian. *Space Demons*. Omnibus/Puffin, 1986.
Rubinstein, Gillian. *Skymaze*. Omnibus/Puffin, 1989.
Salmon, Michael. *The Pirate who Wouldn't Wash*. Lamont Publishing, 1986. **BB**
Sendak, Maurice. *Outside Over There*. Bodley Head, 1981.
Sharp, Alistair. *Moona Park*. Southern Cross Series, Macmillan, 1987.
White. E. B. *Charlotte's Web*. Puffin, 1963.

Assessment and evaluation of modern narratives

This is a suggested summary of aspects you may wish to use for your own particular evaluation needs. They may help you to set specific objectives for this aspect of your language programme. The selection of objectives will be dependent on the language development of the children you teach. Does the student attempt to write in this form? Is the student able to:

- distinguish between contemporary realistic narratives and modern fantasy?
- identify science fiction?
- use the language appropriate to fantasy?
- use imagination to create a fantasy out of a real situation, character or setting?
- explain the features of contemporary realistic narratives?
- identify the problem or issue in the plot?
- build Character Profiles?
- make story maps before writing?
- state what the author would need to know before writing?

BIBLIOGRAPHY

Alderman, Belle. *Best Books For Children*. Ashton Scholastic, 1989.

Brown, Hazel & Cambourne, Brian. *Read and Retell*. Methuen, 1987.

Cambourne, Brian. *The Whole Story—Natural Learning and the Aquisition of Literacy in the Classroom*. Ashton Scholastic, 1988.

Christie, Frances, (ed.). *Children Writing: Study Guide*. Deakin University Press, 1984.

Christie, Frances. *Language Education*. Deakin University Press, 1985.

Collerson, John. (ed.). *Writing For Life*. Primary English Teaching Association, 1988.

Dalton, Joan. *Adventures in Thinking*. Nelson, 1985.

Davidson, M., Isherwood, R. & Tucker, E. *Moving On With Big Books*. Ashton Scholastic, 1989.

Education Department of South Australia. *Writing R-7 Language Arts*. 1979.

Graves, Donald H. *Investigate Non Fiction*. Heinemann, 1989.

Harrison, Ann and McEvedy, M. *From Speech to Writing—Modelling, Evaluating and Negotiating Genres*. Robert Anderson and Associates, 1987.

Hanzl, Anne. *East of the Sun, West of the Moon*. Primary Education, 1986.

Hayhoe, Mike & Parker, Stephen. *Working With Fiction*. Edward Arnold, 1984.

Huck, Charlotte. *Children's Literature in the Elementary School*. 3rd Edition, Holt, Rinehart and Winston, 1961.

Johnson, Terry & Louis, Daphne R. *Literacy Through Literature*. Methuen, 1985.

Kress, Gunther. *Learning to Write*. Routledge and Kegan Paul, 1982.

Martin, J. R. *Factual Writing: Exploring and Challenging Social Reality*. Deakin University Press, 1985.

Painter, Clare & Martin, J. R. (eds). *Writing to mean: Teaching Genres across the Curriculum*. Applied Linguistics Association of Australia Occasional Papers, No. 9, 1986.

Perrine, Laurence. *Sound Sense—An Introduction To Poetry*, Third Edition. Harcourt Brace Jovanovich, 1969.

Pigdon, K. & Woolley, M. 'Getting Inside The Author's Head' in *Towards A Reading Writing Classroom*. Primary English Teaching Association, 1984.

Reid, Ian, (ed.). *The Place of Genres in Learning: Current Debates*. Centres For Studies in Literacy Education, Deakin University, 1987.

Rothery, Joan. *Teaching Writing in the Primary School: A Genre-based Approach to the Development of Writing Abilities*. Department of Linguistics, University of Sydney, 1985.

Rothery, Joan, Martin, J. R. & Christie, Frances. 'Social Processes in Education: A Reply to Sawyer and Watson (and others)' in Reid, Ian (ed.) *A Place of Genre in Learning: Current Debates*. Deakin University, Centre for Studies in Literary Education, 1987.

Southern Cross Resource Book Level Two, Macmillan, 1987.

Stiller, Margaret. *The Joy of Children's Books*. Tiltili Books, 1989.

Thiele, Colin. 'Poetry and the Magic of Words' in *Word Magic Poetry as a Shared Adventure*. Edited by Walter McVitty, Primary English Teaching Association, 1985.

Children's literature referred to in text

Allen, Pamela. *Who Sank the Boat?* Puffin, 1988.

Berndt, Catherine. *Pheasant and Kingfisher.* Bookshelf, Martin Educational, 1987.

Bond, Michael. *A Bear Called Paddington.* Fontana, 1972.

Brinsmead, Hesba. *Longtime Passing.* Golden Press, 1988.

Burmingham, John. *Oi! Get Off Our Train.* Jonathan Cape, 1989.

Byars, Betsy. *After the Goatman.* Puffin, 1978.

Coleridge, Ann. *Longneck's Billabong.* Southern Cross Series, Macmillan, 1987.

Coleridge, Ann. *The Message of the Dance.* Southern Cross Series, Macmillan, 1987.

Collins, Michael, (ed.). *Folk Tales from Asia.* Bookshelf, Martin Educational, 1987.

Dahl, Roald. *The Magic Finger.* Puffin, 1974.

Davidson, Margaret. *Louis Braille—The Boy Who Invented Books for the Blind.* Scholastic, 1971.

Denton, Terry. *Felix and Alexander.* Oxford University Press, 1988.

de Paola, Tomie. *Nana Upstairs & Nana Downstairs.* Methuen, 1985.

Dr Seuss. *The Lorax.* Collins, 1983.

Farber, Norma. *How Does it Feel To Be Old?* Unicorn Book, E. P. Dutton, 1979.

Fox, Mem. *Wilfrid Gordon McDonald Partridge.* Omnibus, 1984.

Fox, Mem. *Sophie.* Drakeford, 1989.

Goble, Paul. *The Girl Who Loved Wild Horses.* Aladdin Books, Macmillan, 1978.

Hackett, J. W. *Bug Haiku.* Japan Publications, 1968.

Harriott, Ted. *Coming Home—a Dog's True Story.* Lynx, 1988.

Howes, Jim. *The Animal Question.* Nelson, 1985.

Howes, Jim. *Five Trees.* Southern Cross Series, Macmillan, 1987.

Howes, Jim. *Down, Roundabout and Up Again.* Southern Cross Series, Macmillan, 1987.

Klein, Robin. *Penny Pollard's Diary.* Oxford University Press, 1983.

Leng, Vikki & Ryles, Judith. *Kids In the Kitchen.* Oxford University Press, 1989.

Lobel, Arnold. *Fables.* Harper and Row, 1980.

Martin, B. *Brown Bear, Brown Bear, What Do You See?* Picture Lions, Collins, 1986.

McCulloch, Deborah & Mansfield, Roger. *See What I Say.* Oxford University Press, 1975.

Ormerod, J. *Moonlight.* Puffin, 1982.

Ormerod, J. *Sunshine.* Puffin, 1982.

Parkes, Brenda. *Red Riding Hood.* Oxford University Press, 1989.

Pearce, Margaret. *The Castle Hill Uprising.* Southern Cross Series, Macmillan, 1987.

Reilly, Pauline. *The Penguin that Walks at Night.* Kangaroo Press, 1985.

Ross, Tony. *Little Red Riding Hood.* Hutchinson Group (Australia), 1978.

Silverstein, Shel. *The Giving Tree.* Jonathan Cape, 1986.

Smyth, Gwenda & James, Ann. *A Pet For Mrs Arbuckle.* Puffin, 1989.

Wildsmith, Brian. *The Lion and the Rat.* Oxford University Press, 1963.

Wildsmith, Brian. *The Hare and the Tortoise.* Oxford University Press, 1966.

Wildsmith, Brian. *The Richman and the Shoe-maker.* Oxford University Press, 1965.

Wildsmith, Brian. *The Miller, the Boy and the Donkey.* Oxford University Press, 1969.

ACKNOWLEDGEMENTS

▼

I wish to thank Marilyn Woolley and Keith Pigdon for working in my classroom and providing the stimulus for me to pursue this interesting exploration of language.

Thank-you to Kay Sagar for all her patient assistance as I prepared this book.

Thank-you to Di Snowball for her encouragement and guidance as I wrote.

A special thank-you to Ken—a willing listener and critical reader.